Kitchen
& Co.

—

Rosie French
& Ellie Grace

Kitchen & Co.

Colourful home cooking
through the seasons

French & Grace
Photography by Laura Edwards

Kyle Books

First published in Great Britain in 2012 by
Kyle Books
23 Howland Street
London W1T 4AY
general.enquiries@kylebooks.com
www.kylebooks.com

10 9 8 7 6 5 4 3 2 1

ISBN 978-0-85783-032-6

Rosie French and Ellie Grace are hereby identified
as the authors of this work in accordance with
Section 77 of the Copyright, Designs and Patents
Act 1988.

Text © 2012 Rosie French & Ellie Grace
Book design © 2012 Kyle Books Limited
Photographs © 2012 Laura Edwards

Project editor: Jenny Wheatley
Art direction & design: Inventory Studio, London
Home economists: Tonia George & Ellie Jarvis
Prop stylists: Rachel Jukes & Lisa Harrison
Editorial assistance: Estella Hung
Production: Gemma John & Nic Jones

A Cataloguing in Publication record for this
title is available from the British Library.

Colour reproduction by Scanhouse in Malaysia
Printed and Bound in China by C&C Offset
Printing Co. Ltd

The kitchen is where our story begins
— Introduction

The kitchen is where our story begins. For those who've followed our blog, you'll know that it was at our kitchen tables, a short cycle from one another in Brixton, south London, that the idea for Salad Club came about. It was here that our first hearty salads were shared and the blog was created as a means of sharing recipes with each other the next day – we had no idea people would actually bother to read it. A month or so later, Ellie's flat above the buzzing market on Electric Avenue became home to our famous secret suppers, where thirty strangers would come to eat three or four courses of homemade food every couple of Saturdays. Donations would be submitted in tobacco tins on the table, wine flowed interminably and our friends would play waitresses. As the calypso and blues hummed on, our bric-a-brac bistro of a restaurant united the city's strangers through food.

Every Saturday that we hosted our supper club was a challenge to our repertoire and an impetus to invent and try out new recipes that would feed large groups from a small galley kitchen. We learned a great deal as we went, some of which is handed down on the following pages. We hope this book will become scuffed and stained on other kitchen tables, however small. Even now, at a new kitchen table at the other end of Brixton, we still use ours as a desk space and meeting place for recipe writing.

We didn't want the title of our book to evoke images of large country kitchens with high ceilings and hanging clusters of pans, or industrial warehouse spaces with light pouring in over a designer Scandinavian table – as much as we like being invited to such places, neither of us live or cook in such places. We live and work in small London flats with kitchens just big enough for a table, and when friends come round it's a matter of squashing up, elbow to elbow, and getting stuck in. Our kitchen tables are covered, from day to day, with unread sections of the weekend newspapers, unpaid bills and glasses destined for the dishwasher.

We don't want to fool you into thinking these spaces are immaculately and religiously wiped down, linen-clothed and gleaming; we don't intend the kitchen tables to be the holy grail of this book. They are where we sit down at the end of a long day with too much wine and a simple supper, or on a weekend morning with more papers destined for the pile, some eggs and lots of coffee. It's where we feel most at home at mealtimes and it's where Salad Club, in all its guises, came to be. From blog to supper club to cookbook and everything that came between.

Limitations of space, money and time have all too often made the traditional dining room a thing of the past. We enjoy a more sociable cooking and eating experience due to open-plan living, which forces us to cook, eat, live and work in one space. Standing at the hob while the people you're feeding crack open the wine and settle in is often cited as one of life's great pleasures. Eating in the kitchen with the cook has gone from being an activity reserved for lowly servants and staff to something highly desirable, hands-on and seductive. Everyone gets to smell and see what's happening at the same time.

Second only to the kitchen table and the company it keeps is the weather. We both love to complain about it, predict it and, most importantly, cook according it. On glum, wet, chilly days when the sun barely rises above the trees, you'll find the kitchen the safest, most logical place to be and a stew of rich, smoky pork the only comfort. Equally, the punchy heat of a cool, crisp radish salad in the middle of a city's summer is all you need to keep your bloodflow stable and your tastebuds alive.

We like to 'cook' in the cold months and 'assemble' when it's hot. Our summers are far too short to be hanging around inside for too long, so you may notice that the kitchen table becomes a little more mobile during summer, when we shuffle out into Ellie's walled garden, spill onto Rosie's rickety allotment furniture or convene on a park bench.

Despite the weather's obvious influence on what we want to cook and eat, we don't have a dogmatically seasonal approach. A cook's instinct will often lead you towards seasonal ingredients without being coerced: winter's crop of starchy, nobbly roots fulfils the innate desire to eat heavily and warmly when it's cold. It all makes (common) sense. However, we also recognise that embellishments here and there from further afield, which may remind us of warmer, sunnier times, are more than welcome in the gloomy months of winter.

It's important to say that we can also be found eating from the fridge or at the kitchen counter – we are untrained cooks with busy lives and do not feel precious or fetishistic about food. We've both made things that have been so

embarrassing as to be binned outright. And we have both invented weird, private combinations of foods that we eat only when alone and in a hurry. Those things haven't made it into the book, but that's not to say we won't go on making them up and scoffing them in private, hoping that no one will ever see.

What's in the cupboard or salad drawer of the fridge is often our starting point. We have well-stocked kitchens with jarred pulses and grains, spices and vinegars in the cupboards and often a bunch of fresh herbs or a corner of white cheese in the fridge. Our cooking comes from being economical and wanting enough for seconds or tomorrow's lunch, knowing that you can invent anything provided your ingredients are good and your imagination willing to take a few chances.

We work and think loosely when it comes to making supper for six friends, calling on spices, grains and vegetables already available to us in order to make it up as we go along. These are the principles of what and how we cook; our cooking has no need for precision – a little too much of this, or less of that won't ruin your supper. We like our food to be healthy but also hearty and robust.

What we've learned is on show in our recipes – our choice of ingredients from a number of countries and cuisines, but none of them impossible to find. We shop every other day (or thereabouts) at our local market, which is a rich source of Middle Eastern, Jamaican and European foods. We know that we're lucky to have this resource, that it isn't the norm, and so we've tried to make each of the recipes super-market-shoppable too.

As we shop, we make forays into ethnic supermarkets, wholefood shops and independent stores where curious and unusual ingredients can be picked up and put aside for later use. Though some of the ingredients may be out of the ordinary, once we have them, they become ever useful or versatile. Often we find something unusual – rose petals, pink peppercorns or rice paper – on shopping trips and buy these for the sake of having a starting point. If either of us opens a cupboard to them several days or weeks later, we'll find a way of working a new recipe around their colour or flavour. This book is about how we eat, and is born out of living above, being fed by – and starting a supper club from – a busy street market.

A word about puddings. Puddings, for us, are a bit of an encumbrance to a good meal. Neither of us has natural aplomb in the art of pudding-making; it's something about

the scientific precision that prohibits quick and easy play with new ideas and styles that puts us off. We realise we can't avoid them, however, and for that reason we've included a few puddings in the Salad Club style. They make no pretenses as to their provenance; they are not especially classy but they save time and are delicious. Our puddings are about minimum effort and maximum impact, and they cannot and should not go wrong.

In the summer of 2011 we took the bold – and slightly mad – move towards having our own kitchen under Salad Club ownership. We'd spent much of the year writing and styling this book and 'going mobile' with our street food venture. It was time to try and stand still (ish) and invite people into our new kind of kitchen.

Uniting the key features of both our home kitchens, we set to work converting a butcher's shop in Brixton Village into a 20-seater kitchen-restaurant. We even went so far as to put our names above it, and have sought to keep intact the friendly, colourful approach to cooking and hosting that was so popular at our Salad Club secret restaurant.

It's been a fantastic journey and we really hope you'll enjoy making your way into and around your own kitchen with this book.

French & Grace

Spring

Spring

There is an endless list of things about which to eulogise when winter releases its grip and surrenders to spring: blossoms bloom, countless woollen layers are removed, windows are left open and you can finally lift your head up for long enough to make eye contact with passers-by rather than hiding inside your collar. Mealtimes start to become more effortless as our kitchen tables loosen up and we stack up our plates in readiness for a more sociable season.

As we push our heaviest pots and pans to the back of the cupboard, slow roasts and stews make way for fish, rare grilled meats and fresh springy salads. Little spoons of this and forkfuls of that fill our plates and are easily scooped up between fingertips and hunks of bread. Winter's heavy reds shuffle over to make room for crisp, cold whites and, as the lighter evenings roll on, we return to a more relaxed way of eating – now in time with the sun's descent – rather than greedily fuelling ourselves in the dark as we must in winter. Everything smells better and tastes fresher as the ground warms up and the days get longer.

We're now able to get back on our bikes, without fear of frostbite, and pop down to the market, or to one another's flats, for a cooking and writing session at the kitchen table. Life suddenly seems to speed up and becomes more flexible in spring – friends need less persuading to trek south for a spontaneous supper and are in no hurry to leave once they're here. As our social lives get busier so, invariably, do our kitchens. Now less obliged to fill and warm our guest's bellies, our focus shifts to filling the table with smaller plates packed with the flavours and colours of the burgeoning season. The euphoria of spring and that extra evening light makes for a more productive kitchen with an increasingly busy and abundant table at its centre.

A Menu for Spring

Breakfast & Brunch
...
Oeufs en Cocotte: 8 Ways

Something Light
...
Crab with Ginger and Spring Onion
Pak Choi Broth
Bruschetta Many Ways
Beef Carpaccio with Dill and Mustard Pesto
Green Lentils with Fresh Thyme, Beetroot and Ricotta
Asparagus, Shallot and Feta Tart
Leek and Gorgonzola Tart
Salmon and Sea Bass Ceviche

Spring Suppers
...
Beefburger Bagel with Beetroot and Caper Salad,
Crispy Fried Onions and Avocado
Barley Risotto with Blue Cheese and Spinach
Maple-glazed Ham Hock with Red Lentil Mash and Savoy Cabbage
Pan-fried Sea Bream with Fennel Gratin
Apple and Fennel Salad with Chorizo
Creamy Chicken, Leeks and Tarragon with Crunchy New Potatoes
Lamb and Date Kofte Kebabs with Halloumi and Tomato Salad
Linguine with Sicilian Pesto

Something Sweet
...
Mascarpone Cheesecake with Nutmeg and Maple Syrup Caramel
Rhubarb and Cassis Tartlets
Carrot, Courgette and Orange Loaf
Chocolate Chip Semifreddo
Mango and Raspberry Lassi

Easy brunch for egg lovers
— *Oeufs en Cocotte: 8 Ways*

These dinky breakfast eggs are just as quick as any other you might make on a Saturday when the time is ripe for a long pot of coffee, a good scour of the papers and a silent glide around the kitchen as you settle into the start of a weekend. Cooked this way, each yolk nestled with its white in the ramekin, we're reminded of hatched Easter eggs in different wrappers; each egg with its own colours and flavours and the decision of those around the table to jump in and take whichever they fancy. Though government guidelines on how many eggs we should be eating changes with the decades, this is one quick breakfast we feel won't be going out of fashion. Whatever the weather, 'EGGS ARE GOOD!'

Each ramekin serves one, with buttered brown toast. The method is pretty much unchanged for each type of egg – it's just a case of putting the initial ingredient in between the tomato purée and egg and then finishing with the others; it just depends how you want it to look. Feel free to play with the ingredients, or to try anything that needs eating from the fridge – we wouldn't expect anyone to make all of these at once; weekend breakfasts aren't meant to be too laborious. We prefer to top the eggs with fresh herbs once out of the oven, but it's up to you.

Serves 8

4 teaspoons tomato purée
Seasonings, as below
8 free range eggs
Few knobs of butter
Salt and pepper

1. Parmesan, breadcrumbs and sage: tomato, grated Parmesan, breadcrumbs, sage
2. Ham and asparagus: ham, few asparagus spears
3. Greek yogurt and paprika with coriander: heaped teaspoon of yogurt in place of the butter, paprika, fresh coriander
4. Sumac, parsley and chilli flakes: sumac, parsley, chilli to taste
5. Sautéed mushrooms and croutons: tomato, mushrooms, croutons
6. Sautéed leeks: leeks cooked in a little butter
7. Anchovy and spring onion: tomato, minced anchovies, spring onion
8. Smoked salmon and dill: smoked salmon, dill

Preheat the oven to 180°C/gas mark 4. Smear a generous half-teaspoon of concentrated tomato purée into the bottom of 8 ramekins and add your chosen seasonings, excluding any fresh herbs. Crack an egg into each ramekin, top with a little butter and season. Fill a baking tray with around 2cm of boiling water from the kettle and place the ramekins in the tray so they're half submerged in the water.

Bake for up to 15 minutes or until the eggs are just set – this will vary quite dramatically between ovens that do or do not have overhead elements so keep an eye on them. Top with the fresh herbs and serve immediately.

A garden lunch for two
— *Crab with Ginger and Spring Onion*

Part of the fun of writing a cookbook – and, of course, where our blog took its starting point – is in expanding our repertoire and making the effort to venture in new directions. Having craved crab on a blustery but sunny spring day, Ellie cycled to the fishmonger's and learned a bit about picking apart a fresh crab for a working lunch with Rosie. If you, too, have just a wooden skewer and a fork to hand you'll get there, but the addition of nutcrackers and a crab picker would probably speed things up. If you're not interested in opening up a crab, or haven't the time, look for a fishmonger who'll sell you one ready prepared.

If rice vinegar isn't within reach, just leave it out. The meat of a female crab with its roe will turn the mix coral pink; we prefer to use a male crab for this reason as he has a lovely silvery white flesh tone, though there's little difference in the taste.

Serves 2

1 crab
1 lime
1 spring onion
Thumb-sized piece of fresh ginger, peeled
Squirt of rice vinegar
Squirt of fish sauce
Glug of sesame oil
½ teaspoon sugar

To serve
Brown toast
Lime wedges

Bring a large pot of salted water to the boil. Add the crab along with a length of lime peel. Boil for 15 minutes, skimming off any scum from the surface.

Thinly slice the white and pale green section of the spring onion into fine lengths, just like those you eat with duck pancakes. Slice the darker green fronds into thin rounds, stopping before it gets woody, and set aside. Add the pale lengths of spring onion to a small bowl and grate in the ginger with a fine zester, reserving a little for serving, so that its juices mix with the onion. Squeeze in the lime juice and add the rice vinegar, fish sauce, sesame oil and sugar. Stir well until the sugar has dissolved.

Lift the crab from the water and sit it on its head. When its cool enough to handle, prise it open from the 'seam' in its shell at its rear end. Use a fork to remove the brown meat from the slimmer part of the shell into a bowl. Remove the legs and crack open to retrieve the white meat. Mix the meats together with a fork and turn with the ginger and spring onion dressing. Serve generously heaped on brown toast and finish with a little lime juice, the greener rings of spring onion and the remaining ginger.

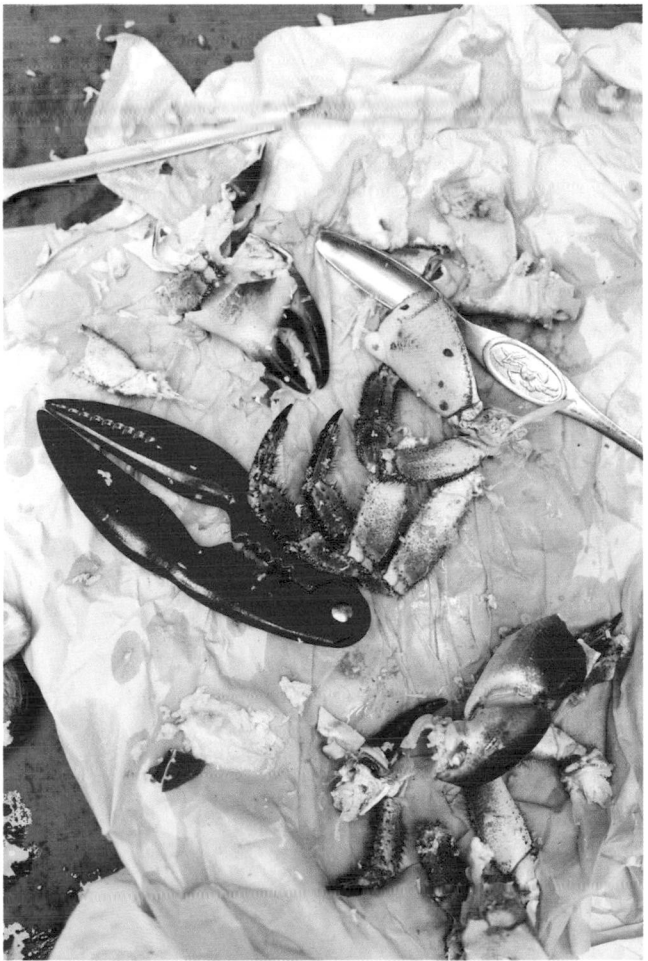

A cleansing spring soup
— *Pak Choi Broth*

This is a soul-warming bowl of hot broth for any tired, run-down or chilly-boned person in need of a bit of fast food and comfort, and most of the ingredients should be in your fridge or cupboard. Having said that, it's not just for the exhausted – it's clean and healthy and offers that satisfying combination of hot and sour flavours tempered nicely by a few quarters of fragrant pak choi, so it'll leave you feeling light and energised. If you can't get hold of pak choi in an oriental supermarket, a handful of glass noodles, bean sprouts, cooked prawns or slices of cooked chicken breast would do well in this simple recipe – just add any or all of them while the liquid simmers.

Serves 1

1 lemongrass stalk
Thumb-sized piece of fresh ginger, peeled
  and finely chopped
1 small red bird's-eye chilli, finely chopped
  or sliced into thin rings (deseeding is
  up to you)
Glug of fish sauce
Juice of half a lime
Dash of soy sauce
Dash of rice vinegar
430ml chicken stock
1 pak choi, cut into quarters

Split open the stalk of lemongrass lengthwise by crushing with the flat of a knife. Cut roughly into thirds and add to a pan with the ginger and chilli. Add the fish sauce, lime juice, soy sauce, vinegar and chicken stock, bring to a boil, then reduce to a simmer. Steam the pak choi above the pan for 3–4 minutes, then plunge into the soup. Continue to simmer for another 15 minutes, then remove the lemongrass. Serve in a deep bowl.

A special Saturday evening with friends
— *Bruschetta Many Ways*

One of the things we like to do as hosts at our supper club is welcome people through the door with a little bit of bread. Not just bread of bread-and-butter fame, but bread with all manner of good, colourful ingredients on top, and a healthy drizzle of flavoursome olive oil and sea salt. Even though making bruschetta in large batches can be stressful – often resulting in burnt forearms and burnt toast if the grill is left unsupervised – it's thoughtful to give your guests the chance to line their stomachs before drinking their way through the night. Anything to get a good supper started.

One of the easiest and most attractive ways of making bruschetta in large numbers is not to worry about precision or exactitude. Just buy a good baguette or ciabatta loaf and a few ingredients for scattering – there's no need to make every one the same. Far better to have a bit of this and a bit of that, to entice people back to the board or plate where they started, and to make your job in the kitchen easier. Just compile as you go – nothing needs to match. Finish a big board of them with a drizzle of quality olive oil and a sprinkling of sea salt.

Ideas for combinations

Mozzarella and olives
Basil, ham and fig vinegar
Ham and olives
Roasted peppers and thyme
Ricotta and pesto
Ham and Pecorino
Mozzarella and chilli
Roasted fennel and goats' cheese
Roasted fennel, olives and capers
Taleggio and pesto
Grilled courgette and tapenade
Garden herbs with mozzarella or tomatoes
Spare fridge ingredients...

Two terrific salads
— *Beef Carpaccio with Dill and Mustard Pesto*
— *Green Lentils with Fresh Thyme, Beetroots and Ricotta*

Beef Carpaccio with Dill and Mustard Pesto

A good fillet of beef is hair-raisingly expensive – so expensive that on a recent trip to our local butcher, Ellie bought two enormous whole fillets without asking the price and weight in advance. When they were handed over at the counter at a cost of £135 (that's with a caterers' discount), she was so embarrassed that she paid up and cycled home in mortified shame. It wasn't until she got home and admitted to herself there was no plausible way of eating it all even between 20 people that she called them up and asked to return half. Even then, you can see it was still a pricey bit of meat. Just beware – if you're ordering your meat over the phone, always ask about the quantities – and prices – before you commit! Thankfully, returning the fillet meant being able to put money towards the rest of the meal's ingredients – without it, we would have been eating an expensive supper of raw beef alone. You can ask your butcher to cut you a section of their fillet – you certainly don't have to buy the whole piece.

Although this is on the far end from frugal, we're believers in spending more money on a little fantastic quality meat for a special occasion. As the slices are very thin, a good-sized fillet will stretch far and wide and with a plate like this, you're guaranteed to satisfy the most carnivorous of meateaters, as well as get more for your money when feeding a larger group. If the idea of raw meat leaves you cold, you could oil and sear the fillet before slicing.

Serves 10

For the beef
1kg beef fillet
Best quality extra virgin olive oil,
  for coating

For the pesto
3 handfuls of pine nuts
Long glug of best olive oil
Heaped teaspoon Dijon mustard
Bunch of dill, finely chopped
Salt and pepper

Lay out a sheet of clingfilm on a clean work surface. Use a sharp knife to slice into the beef fillet on a slight angle, cutting cleanly through the meat as thinly as possible. Lay each slice side by side on the clingfilm and when the sheet is full, place a new sheet over the top. Use a rolling pin to flatten the slices of beef – it doesn't matter if they fray. Transfer the beef to a wide serving platter and cover with a decent layer of olive oil. Continue slicing and layering the beef over two or three platters. Refrigerate until needed and remove at least half an hour before serving.

To make the pesto, whizz together the pine nuts, oil, mustard, dill and seasoning to form a pesto and adjust the seasoning to your taste. Serve in small bowls for guests to spoon over their carpaccio.

Green Lentils with Fresh Thyme, Beetroot and Ricotta

This filling side salad is hugely popular for its clean, earthy and woody flavours and is inspired by Ruth Rogers and Rose Gray of the River Cafe. It's an easy one to prepare at the start of a day's cooking for friends and will keep in the fridge for a day or so, though it is best eaten at its freshest. See if you can find a slice of ricotta at a deli counter rather than the slightly sloppy stuff on offer at supermarkets – the grainy texture and gentle flavour is a real plus. Alternatively, goats' curd makes a wonderful pairing. There's no need to peel the beets if you've scrubbed them well.

Serves 10

2 garlic cloves, peeled
340g dried green lentils
2 large beetroots, topped, tailed and
  scrubbed
Long glug of walnut oil
Few sprigs of fresh thyme, stalks discarded
150g ricotta cheese
Salt and pepper

Put a lidded pan of water on to boil with a pinch of salt and a drop of oil. As it warms, add the garlic cloves. When it comes to a rolling boil, add the lentils and cook to al dente, about 10–15 minutes.

Meanwhile, grate the beetroot into a shallow serving bowl. Toss with the walnut oil and some of the thyme leaves and season generously.

When the lentils are cooked, drain and refresh. Remove the garlic. Add to the beetroot and toss gently, being careful not to colour the lentils too heavily. Taste for seasoning and walnutty-ness, scatter with the rest of the thyme leaves, then lay rough slices of ricotta on top. Drizzle with extra walnut oil just before serving.

A couple of tarts
— *Asparagus, Shallot and Feta*
— *Leek and Gorgonzola*

There's no shame in buying ready-made pastry, especially when you're short of time. Filo is lower in fat than puff and shortcrust and makes an extra crunchy casing for these delicious spring fillings. If you're planning a picnic or having friends over for lunch, a couple of savoury tarts and some salads are sure to go down well.

Asparagus, Shallot and Feta Tart

'Tis the season for cheap asparagus, which is always nice when you want to use a whole bunch of the stuff. If you keep some filo in the freezer you should be able to knock up a version of this tart at quite short notice.

Serves 8

6 sheets filo pastry
Hunk of Parmesan
6 shallots
Knob of butter
Glug of olive oil
1 bunch asparagus (approx 250g)
2 free range eggs
50ml double cream
50ml whole milk
50g feta
Salt and pepper

Preheat the oven to 180°C/gas mark 4. Butter and flour a 25cm tart dish and line with the first sheet of filo. Overlap the next sheet at a different angle so all sides of the dish are covered. Grate over some Parmesan and repeat until you have used all 6 sheets.

Peel the shallots and cut into quarters, lengthways. Heat the butter and oil in a frying pan over a low heat and add the shallots. Cook for 15 minutes, stirring occasionally, until they are starting to soften and take on colour.

Bend each asparagus spear near the base until it snaps and discard the ends. Slice the spears diagonally into roughly 2.5cm long pieces and add them to the pan for about 2 minutes until a slightly paler green, then turn off the heat.

Crack the eggs into a small mixing bowl, add the cream and milk and whisk until combined.

Tip the shallots and asparagus into the pastry, pour in the egg mixture and crumble over the feta. Season lightly and bake for 30 minutes until the tart has puffed up and turned golden on top.

Leek and Gorgonzola Tart

Serves 8

6 sheets filo pastry
6 leeks, washed and trimmed
Knob of butter
Small glass dry white wine
3 extra-large handfuls fresh spinach
75g Gorgonzola
1 tablespoon cream cheese
Salt and pepper

Preheat the oven to 180°C/gas mark 4. Line the tart dish as for the Asparagus, Shallot and Feta Tart, omitting the Parmesan. Slice the leeks into fine rings and sweat with seasoning and butter on a low heat until softened (about 5–10 minutes). Add the wine and let it reduce. Add the spinach and, once wilted, stir in the Gorgonzola and cream cheese. Fill the pastry case and bake for 30 minutes until golden brown.

A fresh and fishy lunch for four
— *Salmon and Sea Bass Ceviche*

When Rosie was pregnant, one of her biggest sacrifices was giving up sashimi. Sometimes all you need in life is a plate of raw fish and a wasabi rush up the nose to sort everything out. Nine months without a sushi fix was tough.

One way around this problem (please consult your doctor first) was to 'cook' the fish in citrus juice, South American style. Just like sushi, ceviche needs spankingly fresh fish and therefore a good fishmonger. We like the combination of oily salmon with creamy bass but you can stick to one fish or go for any combination you like. Bream, tuna, brill and sea trout all work brilliantly, too.

It's up to you how long you leave the fish to 'cook'. Just keep tasting until you approve. Most modern versions of this dish are served up instantly but this is a more traditional Peruvian version whose piquant flavours appreciate the time to fight and eventually make up, softening the onions and turning the fish opaque in the process.

Serves 4

Juice of 3 limes and zest of 1
Juice and zest of 1 clementine
½ red onion, very finely sliced
½ red chilli, deseeded and very finely sliced
Large handful of coriander, very finely chopped
½ teaspoon caster sugar
1 tablespoon soy sauce
1 tablespoon olive oil
1 salmon fillet
1 sea bass fillet

To serve
Sesame oil
Small handful of coriander, very finely chopped

Use your sharpest knife to slice everything (but the fish) as finely and cleanly as possible.

Place all the ingredients, minus the fish, in a bowl. Dice the salmon and bass fillets into roughly 1cm cubes and add to the bowl. Stir gently to combine and let the fish and onions 'cook' in the citrus for at least 5 minutes (adjust time to taste). Serve in small bowls with a tiny dash of sesame oil and a little more fresh coriander.

Avocado with Chilli
This is not a full-on recipe but a quick aside to the ceviche – all you need is a sharp knife. In Chile, where Rosie lived for a few months, avocado is often included in the ceviche mix. Just take 2 ripe avocados, thickly sliced, drizzled with a little olive oil and sprinkle with salt, pepper and a few chilli flakes. Serve on the side.

An alternative burger and salad for the season's first barbecue
— *Beefburger Bagel with Beetroot and Caper Salad, Crispy Fried Onions and Avocado*

This is a monster of a burger. And now that it's tried and tested, there seems little point in going back to the regular pairing of cheese and tomato. The bagels in this recipe are Brick Lane's most famous. Every Sunday, queues snake out of the two bakeries at the north end of the street and customers step out of the hot shop fronts with buns stuffed with tangy mustard and salt beef or thick cream cheese and smoked salmon. Having bought a too-large paper bag of plain ones I realised they quickly had to find a home in my stomach. It turns out they hold the weight of a burger better than a seeded bun and have a pleasing touch of the Yorkshire pudding about them when soaked with mustard and beef juices. What could possibly be better? When it comes to English mustard, only Colman's will do – mixing it yourself from powder will have the sharpest, most eye-watering effect, which is just what we're going for. This recipe can be made on a hob or barbecue, depending on the weather and your expertise.

Heat a little oil on low in a frying pan and add the onion, stirring until brown and crisped. Place the bagel halves under a gentle grill or at the edge of the barbecue, taking care to turn and remove when ready.

Push the onion to the edge of the pan, oil and season the burgers on both sides and turn the heat to high. Add the burgers to the centre of the pan and press down with a fish slice. Cook on both sides for 5 minutes without moving – shorter if the burger isn't very fat or you prefer your beef rare.

Meanwhile, toss the grated beetroot in a bowl with the olive oil, mustard, lemon juice and capers. As soon as the burgers are ready, stack the dressed beetroot on the bagel bases and top with the burgers and avocado slices. Finish with the crispy fried onions and the bagel tops. Eat quickly and messily with an ice-cold beer.

Serves 4

For the burgers
600g minced beef
Handful of breadcrumbs
Handful of fresh thyme leaves, picked
Couple of dashes of Worcestershire sauce
Salt and pepper

For the accompaniments
Olive oil, for frying and dressing
1 large white onion, peeled and sliced
4 bagels, halved
1 large beetroot, scrubbed and grated
1 teaspoon hot English mustard powder, ready-mixed
Juice of ½ a lemon
1 heaped teaspoon capers, drained and rinsed
1 avocado, peeled, stoned and sliced

Start by mixing the burger ingredients together in a bowl, using your hands to combine. We sometimes make breadcrumbs to keep in the freezer when there's a surplus of bread about, but with none to hand, it's easy to quickly toast a slice of bread and either whizz it in the food processor or crumble it by hand. Shape the mixture into patties and refrigerate for 30 minutes.

A simple moreish meal for two
— Barley Risotto with Blue Cheese and Spinach

This recipe was born out of a gentle spring evening with a few fridge ingredients knocking around and the prospect of a meal for one alone at the kitchen table. Sometimes you come up with the best ideas when you're in your own company. Even though the recipe serves 2 people, I ended up eating the whole pot. I used barley because I didn't have enough risotto rice in the cupboard – feel free to use either, though barley is a far cheaper option. As for blue cheese, use whatever's available to you – my favourite is Saint Agur, available in all big supermarkets. Serve with a bitter salad of escarole or radicchio and a glass of crisp white wine.

Serves 2

1 small red onion, peeled and sliced
Small knob of butter
3 handfuls of barley
1 glass of white wine
300ml vegetable stock
2 large handfuls of fresh spinach
2 tablespoons cream cheese
50g blue cheese
Juice and zest of ½ a lemon
½ spring onion, very finely sliced (optional)
Salt and pepper

Sweat the onion with the butter until soft and golden. Add the barley and stir to coat for a minute. Pour in the white wine and half the stock. Keeping the lid off, turn the heat to high, bring to the boil, then reduce to a simmer. Stir occasionally and gradually add the remaining stock as it is absorbed. Cook until the barley is al dente and the liquid has reduced. Add the spinach to the pan and fold in with a wooden spoon or fork as soon as it starts to wilt. Quickly introduce the two cheeses and stir to melt entirely. Season to taste. Serve immediately with a little lemon juice, zest and the spring onion, if you're using it.

Supper enough for leftovers
— *Maple-glazed Ham Hock with Red Lentil Mash and Savoy Cabbage*

Ham hock – or the less sexy gammon knuckle – is one of the cheapest and tastiest bits of pig you can get at your butcher (which sort of makes up for the expense of the maple syrup!). Ask for an unsmoked knuckle, which is usually sealed and lightly preserved, hence the need to rinse before cooking. Even though the ham hock is delicious fresh from the oven, try to resist eating it all. It would be criminal not to save a few chunks of dark pink meat for your lunchtime sandwich. Just be sure to treat it to plenty of English mustard, your favourite chutney and a handful of peppery leaves.

Red lentils make a great alternative to mash when you're not in the mood for potatoes. They cook quickly and have a similar starchiness but with more texture and bite. A gentle, healthy and economical storecupboard accompaniment.

Serves 2 with leftovers

For the ham
1.5kg ham hock
2 litres cider
2 fresh bay leaves
100g maple syrup
Sea salt

For the lentil mash
1 medium red onion, finely sliced
Olive oil, for frying
Small handful thyme leaves
100g red lentils
Small knob of butter

For the cabbage
½ head Savoy cabbage
1 tablespoon red wine vinegar

Rinse the ham hock under cold running water and place in a large pan. Empty the cider into the pan and, if the hock isn't completely submerged, top up with cold water. Throw in the bay leaves and bring to the boil. Reduce to a gentle simmer, cover and leave for 2 hours. Turn off the heat, remove the lid and let the contents of the pan cool.

Preheat the oven to 190°C/gas mark 5. Remove the ham hock from the cider and score the fat with a sharp knife in both directions. Place in a deep-sided baking tray and cover on all sides with the maple syrup and some generous pinches of sea salt, barely crushed.

Roast for 45 minutes, basting when you remember, until dark brown and crisped at the edges. Remove, cover with foil and a tea towel and leave to rest while you get on with the side dishes.

To make the mash, first boil the kettle. Fry the onion in a saucepan with a little olive oil until soft, add the thyme and lentils and stir for a minute or so. Pour in enough boiled water to just cover the lentils and leave to simmer gently for 10–15 minutes until most of the water has been absorbed. Meanwhile thickly slice the cabbage and place in a steamer. Either place the steamer over the lentil pan or over a pan of boiling water and leave to steam for 5 minutes while you uncover the ham hock and take it to the table on the board to hack into chunks – the meat shouldn't need much encouragement to fall from the bone.

Just before serving, add the butter to the lentils and the vinegar to the cabbage. Delicious with a cold glass of wheat beer or a pint of ale.

A fine fish supper
— Pan-fried Sea Bream with Fennel Gratin

Forget cod and haddock, sea bream is the king of white fish (closely followed by skate). All it needs is a very short spell in some hot bubbling butter and you have yourself a fine fish supper. This gratin recipe also works well with endive. The breadcrumbs used here are a great way to use up stale bread. Rather than throwing stale bread away, blitz it into crumbs, drizzle with oil (adding some woody herbs such as rosemary or thyme, if you like) and store in an airtight container, or in the freezer, until you need them.

Serves 2

For the gratin
2 large or 3 small fennel bulbs
1 tablespoon capers, rinsed and drained
Zest of ½ a lemon
100g breadcrumbs
Glug of olive oil
Parsley, finely chopped
2 garlic cloves, sliced

For the bream
25g butter
1 tablespoon olive oil
2 black or sea bream fillets (approx 100g each)
Salt and pepper

Preheat the oven to 180°C/gas mark 4. To make the gratin slice each fennel bulb into quarters lengthways and blanch in boiling water for 5 minutes. Drain and tip into a baking tray. Mix all the other ingredients together vigorously with your hands and tip over the fennel. Bake for 25–30 minutes.

When the gratin only has 5 minutes to go, put a couple of plates in the oven and heat the butter and olive oil in a frying pan over a medium heat until bubbling. Gently slide in the bream, skin-side down, and cook for 2–3 minutes (or until the skin has crisped). Spoon some melted butter over the flesh and sprinkle with salt and pepper, then gently flip the fillets and cook for another 1–2 minutes. Tip onto the warm plates and serve with the gratin and some wilted spinach, chard or spring greens.

Late lunch or early supper
— *Apple and Fennel Salad with Chorizo*
— *Creamy Chicken, Leeks and Tarragon with Crunchy New Potatoes*

One day you're up, the next you're down. A few weeks ago we were pushing our winter clothes to the back of the wardrobe and confidently leaving our flats without a jacket. Things have changed this week and, while the allotment is grateful for the rain, we're not so thrilled to be digging out our warm jumpers and climbing into cold sheets at night. However, we can find solace in returning to something warming and comforting for one of those slow Sunday afternoons with a few bottles of wine, some good music playing and the shared sense that there's nowhere better to be at the end of a damp spring weekend than inside and around the kitchen table.

Apple and Fennel Salad with Chorizo
You'll have already noticed, we're sure, that at Salad Club we fly the chorizo flag high and proud. Celebrated for its vibrant flavour, it's not hard to find a partner for the versatile, spicy sausage much beloved by us and Spaniards alike! Pairing its punchy earth colours with pale slivers of raw, lemon-dressed apple and fennel turns this often heavy sausage into a fresh and beautiful spring starter or side salad. It also goes down well with grilled white fish or a mezze of mixed salads. Serve with chilled Prosecco for a real treat.

Serves 6

3 fennel bulbs, very finely sliced, fronds
  reserved
1 crisp apple (Cox or Granny Smith — or
  whatever you prefer), very finely sliced
Juice of ½ a lemon
100g good cooking chorizo, cut into 1cm slices

Combine the fennel, apple and lemon juice in a serving bowl. Fry the chorizo on a medium heat in a dry pan until browned and oozing, no more than a couple of minutes on each side. Lift from the pan straight onto the salad, following with the sausage juices. Finish with a few of the fennel fronds and eat immediately.

Creamy Chicken, Leeks and Tarragon with Crunchy New Potatoes

Serves 6

For the chicken
12 chicken thighs
Olive oil, for frying
2 leeks, chopped into roughly 2.5cm rounds
Large glass of dry white wine
1 litre chicken stock
Large handful of tarragon leaves, chopped
150ml double cream
2 tablespoons grain mustard
10—15 fresh pea pods (optional), shelled
Salt and pepper

For the potatoes
600g waxy new potatoes
Large glug olive oil
Juice and zest of 1 lemon
Large pinch uncrushed sea salt

Preheat the oven to 180°C/gas mark 4. Season the chicken well and heat a little olive oil in a wide flameproof casserole with a lid. Brown the chicken thighs all over until the skin is well crisped, then set aside.

Add a splash more olive oil to the pan if needed and gently fry the leeks for about 5 minutes until starting to soften. Pour in the white wine and scrape any tasty bits stuck to the bottom of the pan. Return the chicken to the casserole, add the stock and half the tarragon. Bring to the boil, cover and transfer to the oven for 30–40 minutes.

Meanwhile prepare the potatoes. Scrub any mud, cut into bite-size pieces and add to a pan of salted boiling water. Boil for about 10 minutes or until soft to the point of a knife. Drain and, while still steaming, tip into a baking tin, drizzle with oil, squeeze over the lemon juice and throw over the sea salt. Bake on a shelf above the chicken for 25–30 minutes.

Remove the chicken from the oven and stir in the cream, mustard, fresh peas and remaining tarragon. Replace the lid and put the casserole on the table ready to serve. Remove the potatoes from the oven, grate over the lemon zest and take the tin to the table.

The proof is in the pudding
— Mascarpone Cheesecake with Nutmeg and Maple Syrup Caramel

While the list of ingredients may look long, cheesecake is an easy pudding to make (trust us, we're not good at baking), and a popular one, too. There's something very satisfying about sinking your teeth into the sweet-savoury tang of the filling and its partner, and the slightly salty biscuit base. If you can't be faffed to stand at the hob with the caramel, serve with maple syrup instead.

Serves 8

For the base
200g ginger biscuits
200g oat biscuits
75g unsalted butter
Pinch of sea salt

For the filling
500g mascarpone
150ml double cream
200g cream cheese
1 tablespoon icing sugar, sifted
Juice of 2 limes

For the topping
Ground nutmeg, to dust (or freshly grated
  if you have whole nutmegs)
25g butter
100g maple syrup
Splash of double cream

Put the biscuits into a sealed plastic bag and crush to coarse crumbs with a rolling pin (or whizz in a food processor). Melt the butter and add to a mixing bowl along with the biscuits and a splash of cold water. Mix well, then press firmly with your knuckles into a loose-based cake tin. Refrigerate for at least 30 minutes to set.

Rinse the mixing bowl and add the filling ingredients. Blend together and taste. Spread on top of the biscuit base with a spatula and return to the fridge until needed.

Fifteen minutes before serving, remove the cake from the fridge and dust with a generous layer of nutmeg. Heat the butter and maple syrup in a pan over a low heat until melted, stirring a little as you go. When it's reached caramel consistency, add a splash of cream, stir to combine and serve with the cheesecakes. There'll be more than enough for leftovers too.

A weeknight kebab without the hangover
— *Lamb and Date Kofte Kebabs*
— *Mango and Raspberry Lassi*

Lamb and Date Kofte Kebabs

More often than not the need for a kebab strikes at around 2am after an especially lengthy visit to the pub. The joy of making them at home, however, means you can keep track of exactly what's going into the pitta pockets and avoid the guilty remembrance of last night's antics when you wake up. These make a great weeknight supper at the kitchen table, sober or not.

We recommend having a supply of quality pittas in your freezer (a Middle Eastern brand if you can find them). When the fridge is bare you can toast them straight from frozen, whiz up some hummus (see page 60), and have yourself an instant, satisfying snack.

You can also prise them open with a skewer or sharp knife and stuff them with charred meat, oozing cheese, salad and yogurt as I'm about to do. If you're having a barbecue these work wonderfully over coal too.

Serves 4 (makes 8 kebabs)

For the tomato salad
4 medium vine-ripened tomatoes, sliced
   or quartered
Large handful of parsley, finely chopped
1 red chilli, deseeded and finely chopped
1 tablespoon olive oil
Salt and pepper

For the kofte
2 tablespoons couscous
250g minced lamb
5 Medjool dates, stoned and finely chopped
Handful dill, finely chopped
Handful mint leaves, finely chopped
1 free range egg
Large pinch salt and pepper
1 tablespoon groundnut oil

To serve
4 white pittas
8 slices halloumi
4 tablespoons natural yogurt
4 handfuls of peppery salad leaves

Mix all the ingredients for the tomato salad together so the salt has time to draw out the tasty tomato juices.

To make the kofte, put the couscous in a bowl and just cover with boiling water. Cover the bowl with a plate. Put the lamb, chopped dates, herbs, egg and seasoning in a large bowl, fork in the cooked couscous and mix everything together with your hands. Mould roughly into 8 sausage (kofte) shapes and flatten lightly between your palms.

Heat up a griddle pan over a medium-high heat and pour in the groundnut oil. When the pan is hot, add the kofte and push down lightly so they charr well. Turn the heat down and cook for 6–8 minutes each side, until dark brown and cooked through. Remove from the pan and keep warm.

Toast the pittas and open up the long side with a sharp knife or metal skewer. Put each pitta on a plate ready to fill and serve.

Turn the heat back up under the griddle. Add the halloumi, leave for 1 minute then turn and cook for another minute until charred all over and soft within.

Fill each pitta with 2 kofte, 2 slices of halloumi, some tomato salad, a tablespoon of yogurt and a handful of leaves. Serve immediately with napkins.

Mango and Raspberry Lassi

After a hearty meal we often want a hit of sweetness without the burden of a heavy pudding. Whizzing up a refreshing lassi is a great way to end a meal, especially if you need to cool people down after a chilli-laden menu.

Enough for 4 small tumblers
1 mango, flesh only**
100g raspberries
4 tablespoons natural yogurt
Juice of half a lime
1½ tablespoons golden caster sugar
150ml whole milk
Dash of single or double cream (optional)
Lime zest, to serve

**See page 75 for tips on how to skin a mango.

Simply blitz the ingredients, except the lime zest, in a blender and serve over ice in glass tumblers with a little lime zest on top.

Our first spring supper next to open windows
— Linguine with Sicilian Pesto

We were blessed with a long, premature heat wave this spring and how better to spend an unexpectedly balmy evening than to pretend you're in Sicily?! Three of us pushed up close to the open kitchen windows so as not to miss one gust of warm breeze, very cold white wine in hand and forks at the ready.

It's easy to overload on basil pesto. We both tend to go through phases of eating and craving nothing else until we overdo it and have to leave it alone for a few months. This Sicilian pesto recipe is completely different, with dirtier, more pungent notes. The delicious sweetness from the sultanas works wonders with the salty anchovies and capers. A perfect, quick supper for a warm night.

Serves 3

380g linguine
2 tablespoons sultanas
6 anchovy fillets
1 tablespoon capers, rinsed and drained
4 garlic cloves, peeled and roughly sliced
2 tablespoons pine nuts
Juice and zest of ½ a lemon
6 tablespoons olive oil
Pepper
Large chunk of Parmesan, to serve

Bring a large pan of salted water to a vigorous boil over a high heat and add the linguine.

Soak the sultanas in warm water for a couple of minutes, drain and add to a mortar with the anchovies, capers, garlic, pine nuts and lemon zest. Grind to a rough paste, loosen with the lemon juice and olive oil and add a few grinds of black pepper.

Test the pasta and once al dente, drain (reserving some of the water) and return to the pan, off the heat. Quickly pour over the pesto and a good splash of the cooking water, toss well and serve on a platter in the centre of the table. We never bother grating Parmesan in advance – most people prefer to do it themselves at the table and save you the hassle. *Buon appetito.*

Sweet little things from our market stall
— Rhubarb and Cassis Tartlets
— Carrot, Courgette and Orange Loaf

Towards the end of spring, when the weather was starting to hot up and we were itching to get out and talk to our customers again, we decided to invest in our very own stall and get a pitch at our local farmers' market selling a selection of five or six seasonal salads and a couple of sweet options. Despite our lack of baking prowess, the sweet things always seem to sell well. Here are a couple of guests to the stall.

Rhubarb and Cassis Tartlets
We accidentally bought puff rather than shortcrust pastry for these but they turned out rather well and our customers adored them. Feel free to use shortcrust pastry for a more traditional tartlet. If you're making these to eat at home, a dollop of crème fraîche wouldn't go amiss.

Makes 24

1 sheet ready-made puff or shortcrust pastry
3 sticks rhubarb
1 tablespoon vanilla sugar
1 tablespoon cassis
200g unsalted butter
150g caster sugar
200g ground almonds
2 free range eggs

Preheat the oven to 180°C/gas mark 4. Roll out your pasty to 1cm thickness and cut out discs with a large circular cookie cutter. Grease your smallest tartlet tins or the insides of a muffin tray and line with the pastry discs.

Cut each rhubarb stalk in half lengthways and cut each half into roughly 2.5cm long slices on a diagonal. Put the slices in a bowl with the vanilla sugar and cassis and set aside for at least 10 minutes.

Beat together the butter, sugar, ground almonds and eggs by hand or in a food processor until smooth and creamy. Spoon the mixture into the pastry cases to roughly three quarters full. Arrange 4 or 5 rhubarb pieces on top of each tart and push them down lightly until half submerged.

Bake for 25–30 minutes until risen and golden brown. Leave to cool before serving.

Carrot, Courgette and Orange Loaf
This is a great way to use up a glut of courgettes and, as cakes go, it's not too high in sugar either. Feel free to leave out the icing for a more wholesome teatime treat. You can also play around with the courgette to carrot ratio depending on your stocks.

Makes 2 small loaves

For the cake
200g courgette, grated
100g carrot, grated
2 large free range eggs
150ml vegetable oil
200g soft brown sugar
250g self-raising flour
½ teaspoon bicarbonate of soda
1 teaspoon baking powder
Pinch of salt
Juice and zest of ½ an orange

For the icing
250g Greek yogurt
6 tablespoons icing sugar, sifted
Zest of half an orange

Preheat the oven to 180°C/gas mark 4. Squeeze any excess water out of the courgettes and set aside with the carrots. In a large bowl beat the eggs, oil and sugar together then sift in the flour, bicarbonate of soda, baking powder and salt and beat until combined. Stir in the courgettes and carrots and add the orange juice and zest.

Divide the cake mixture between 2 small loaf tins and bake for 30 minutes until golden and firm to the touch. Leave to cool, then turn out and ice, if desired.

To make the icing, mix together the yogurt, icing sugar and some of the orange zest. Try not to stir the icing too much as it will become too loose. Refrigerate for as long as possible to help it firm up before using to ice the cake.

Half frozen, half the fuss
— *Chocolate Chip Semifreddo*

Rosie has been trying to master this recipe since first sampling the semifreddo at a remote *rifugio* high up in the lakes of the Italian Apennines. The beauty of semifreddo, like an Indian kulfi, is that it doesn't require any churning or supervision, just a little advanced planning so it can set in the freezer overnight. As with so many puddings, it makes for a fair bit of washing up but it's worth it.

Serves 6

3 free range eggs, separated
75g caster sugar
300g whipping cream
Seeds from 1 vanilla pod
50g good-quality dark chocolate, plus extra
  to serve
6 Italian-style biscotti (optional), plus
  extra to serve

Whisk together the egg yolks and sugar until creamy and pale. In a separate bowl, whisk the egg whites until they form stiff peaks. In your largest bowl, lightly whip the cream until soft peaks form and stir in the vanilla seeds. Now stir the egg yolk mixture into the cream with a metal spoon and then gently fold in the egg whites.

Chop the chocolate and biscotti with a sharp knife into chunks and gently stir into the mixture.

Line a medium-sized plastic lidded container with clingfilm. Pour in the mixture and put in the freezer for at least 12 hours. If you remember, move the semifreddo to the fridge an hour before serving (if you forget just give it 10 minutes out of the freezer to melt a bit). Spoon into tumblers or bowls with a few fresh scrapings of dark chocolate and some crumbled biscotti.

Summer

Summer

Oh wonderful elusive summer, with your long days, warm nights and ice-cold beers. Why are you so short? We've barely had time to polish our sunglasses and already you're threatening to leave us here in the gloom while you swan off somewhere hotter.

Few of us can resist the call of the sunshine and yet the English summer is more written about than a reality – it's one of literature's most called-on fantasies and marketable exports! If you're not careful, it can pass you by in a flash so you'll need to grab it while it's hot. Cook outside whenever you can (in a garden, on a city rooftop, perched on a balcony, in a park or even just by an open window), and focus on compiling fresh, colourful ingredients with the minimal amount of fuss. The summer is when Salad Club gets to step up onto its soapbox and proclaim loud and proud the ease, value and beauty of assembling plates of food to be eaten in the fresh air. In just the same way that life seems freer and looser, so too are our eating habits – thankful at last to leave the oven off and sup on cool drinks.

A chunk of this chapter was written and photographed on a trip to Tuscany where it was impossible not to be inspired by the abundance of fresh ingredients and the blazing sun. We love Italian food and the recipes we've discovered on our travels permeate every chapter of this book, particularly this one.

There's nothing easier than turning grains with good olive oil, a little sea salt and fresh herbs and white cheese, or grilling a piece of fish on the barbecue and drizzling over a quickly pounded dressing. Full of the ease and requiescence, we must grab this sweet, precious season while we can.

A Menu for Summer

Breakfast & Brunch

...

Goats' Cheese and Herb Frittata with Chilli
Tuscan Sausages with Eggy Bread and Soft Red Onions

Lunch / Something on the Side

...

Green Beans with Sun-Blushed Tomatoes and Crushed Garlic served
with Baked Taleggio and Crunchy Toast
Braised Lettuce with Peas, Bacon and Shallots
Croque Madame
Mezze Meal
Gazpacho
Orecchiette with Anchovies, Baby Tomatoes and Basil
Chicken with Yogurt and Capers
Coronation or Royal Wedding Chicken
Cucumber and Carrot Salad with Sesame and Chilli
Radicchio, Pear and Gorgonzola Salad
Prosciutto, Melon and Spinach

On the Grill

...

Tagliata con Rucola
Mango Salsa
Chilli and Lime Corn on the Cob
Chargrilled Peppers and Courgettes with Basil and Garlic Oil
Lamb Cutlets with Warm, Creamy Flageolet Beans and Baba Ghanoush

In the Oven

...

Pizzettas

On the Hob

...

Courgette, Sage and Parmesan Risotto

Something Sweet

...

Fresh Berry Ices
Grilled Peaches in Wine
Chocolate Espresso Mousse
Honey, Almond and Polenta Cake

Late breakfast on a summer's weekend
— *Goats' Cheese and Herb Frittata with Chilli*

Frittata is the Italians' unflippable cousin of the Spanish omelette and, unlike the Spanish and French varieties, this one is finished under the grill. We've added potatoes for a light brunch or late breakfast but softened red and yellow peppers with a pinch or two of smoked paprika would be a good alternative.

Serves 4–6

4 shallots, peeled and finely sliced
Knob of butter
2 medium potatoes, scrubbed and thickly sliced
   (or better still use a handful of summer
   Jersey Royals)
6 free range eggs
75g goats' cheese, sliced
Handful of fresh herbs (e.g. mint, parsley and
   thyme), chopped
Pinch of chilli flakes or sumac (or both)
Salt and pepper

Preheat the grill. Sweat the shallots in the butter in a large frying pan. Add the potatoes and cook until golden brown, turning frequently and adding a little oil if needed. Season. Whisk the eggs in a bowl and pour over the potatoes, allowing them to find their way around and settle into the pan. Work around the edge with a fish slice as it cooks, loosening to check the bottom is cooking rather than catching. Do not pull the eggs around with the slice as you would with a French omelette – allow everything to cook together in one piece. When just the top remains to be cooked, lay slices of goats' cheese on top of the frittata and scatter with half the herbs and a pinch of chilli flakes and/ or sumac. Place under the grill and keep an eye on it while it sets and the cheese starts to melt. Remove from the oven, sprinkle over the remaining herbs and cut into wedges.

The full Italian
— *Tuscan Sausages with Eggy Bread and Soft Red Onions*

Not the lightest of breakfasts but more of a hefty brunch to fuel a long walk or some other mildly strenuous exertion. Get the best-quality sausages and eggs you can find and give the onions plenty of time to soften and sweeten while you lose yourself in the papers and sip your coffee.

Serves 8

2 red onions, finely sliced
2 tablespoons white wine vinegar
1 heaped teaspoon caster sugar
Knob of butter
2 x 500g rings Tuscan or Cumberland
    sausage
Glug of olive oil
2 free range eggs
Splash of milk
Pinch of fresh rosemary, chopped
8 slices of day-old bread
Salt and pepper

Put the onions into a small saucepan with the vinegar, sugar and butter. Cover and leave to sweat over the lowest heat for about 30 minutes, stirring occasionally.

Once the onions are on, fry the sausages over a medium heat or roast in the oven at 200°C/gas mark 6 with a small glug of olive oil.

Whisk the eggs, milk, rosemary and seasoning together in a shallow bowl. Submerge each slice of bread in the egg mixture until well soaked and stack the slices up in the bowl, ready for the pan.

When the onions have about 5 minutes left to cook, add a small glug of olive oil to a non-stick frying pan over a medium heat and tip in the eggy bread (along with any excess egg from the bowl). Fry on both sides until browned and crisp.

Serve with the onions scattered over the eggy bread and with some of Rosie's Tomato Chilli Jam (see page 101) if you have a jar knocking around.

A quick summer meal fresh from the market
— *Green Beans with Sun-blushed Tomatoes and Crushed Garlic Served with Baked Taleggio and Crunchy Toast*

We're so accustomed to eating over-boiled beans as a grey accompaniment to grey roast meat that it's easy to forget how beautiful they look in a bowl, tossed well with a few other simple ingredients. There's not much that they won't go well with as their lithe pods soak up all sorts of flavours and will happily sit around without wilting on a warm day. They're also delicious quickly blanched and added in halves to a cool and crunchy salad. Be sure to boil quickly followed by a cold shock under a running tap if you want to keep their colour.

Serves 4

580g green beans, topped and tailed
  (buy a mix of green and yellow if you can)
200g Taleggio
Long glug of best olive oil
Pepper
Juice of ½ a lemon
Large handful of sun-blushed tomatoes
Handful of fresh basil, plus extra for serving
1 large garlic clove, crushed
Pecorino, for shaving
4 slices rustic bread

Preheat the oven to 150°C/gas mark 2. Plunge the beans into a pot of salted, furiously boiling water and cook for about 10 minutes until al dente. Drain and refresh immediately to maintain their colour.

Put the Taleggio rind-side up into a tight-fitting ovenproof dish or bowl (so that it doesn't spread out too far). Bake for 5–10 minutes, keeping an eye on it as it melts – a little bubbling is good. While the cheese bakes, add a glug of oil to a deep serving bowl along with the pepper, lemon juice, tomatoes and basil. Add the crushed garlic to the bowl and whisk together with a fork. Throw in the beans, toss well and shave over a generous amount of salty Pecorino. Toast or grill the bread until crispy.

Finish the salad with more basil and serve with the Taleggio and crusty toast.

Something on the side
— Braised Lettuce with Peas, Bacon and Shallots

There's something autumnal about this side dish, which goes well with all manner of grilled and roasted cuts of lamb. Bring it back to a cooler summer evening by using fresh podded peas if you can find them – a sweet treat of the season – and serve with lamb chops or grilled fish. A crumbling of feta on top would make a quick supper in itself.

Serves 2

4 shallots, peeled and finely chopped
Small knob of butter
Drizzle of olive oil
75g pancetta or smoked bacon, diced
Splash of white wine vinegar
Handful of fresh peas
2 or 3 heads of gem lettuce, leaves separated
   and washed
Flat leaf parsley, chopped, for scattering
Salt and pepper

Soften the shallots in the butter and oil over a low heat. Once the edges have turned a golden brown, season and add the pancetta. Cook until the pancetta is golden brown and add a splash of vinegar to deglaze the pan. Add the peas and lettuce and turn quickly with tongs. As soon as the leaves start to wilt (they should still retain some bite), remove from the pan and place on a serving plate. Scatter with chopped parsley and serve immediately.

From Paris with love
— *Croque Madame*

Ooh la la, it's time for a sandwich, and a diva of a sandwich at that. Don't be put off by the tourist trap versions of these you see near the Gare du Nord in Paris. When done properly at home, a Croque Madame can be the egg-crowned queen of bread-based meals. Treat yourself to good bread and *bon ouefs, s'il vous plaît.*

Makes 1 large sandwich

2 large slices of sturdy white bread
   (sourdough works well)
2–3 slices quality cooked ham
50g of your favourite melting cheese
   (Emmental, Comté, Cheddar and mozzarella
   are all good)
Pinch of thyme leaves
1 free range egg
1 large lettuce leaf

Preheat the grill to hot. Cut a hole out of the centre of one slice of bread. Place both slices under the grill, turning once, until lightly toasted on both sides. Top the complete slice with ham, cheese and a few thyme leaves and return to the grill, on a low shelf, allowing the cheese to melt.

Put the other slice in a non-stick frying pan over a medium heat and crack the egg into the hole. Push the sides of the bread down with a spatula so the egg doesn't escape.

Once the egg is cooked and the cheese has melted, you're ready to compile your Croque! Top the melted cheese with the lettuce, then carefully slide on your egg-filled slice. *Bon appetite,* Madame.

A mezze meal for scooping up with bread
— *Minted Pea and Pecorino Dip; Butterbean and Rosemary Hummus; Borlotti with Feta and Olives; Sour Cream, Spring Onion and Garlic Dip*

Summer calls for everything to be easy. Better to minimise time in the kitchen so as to maximise time outside. Most of our summer eating involves chasing the last bit of blended hummus from a plate of different salads and dips with thick bread, toast or pitta. Cooling mint, yogurt and tahini are among the best of aides in surviving a scorching heatwave.

Minted Pea and Pecorino Dip

```
3 large handfuls fresh peas (use thawed
    frozen peas if you have to, though they
    will impart a  very quirky sweetness!)
Handful of fresh mint, roughly chopped
Glug of best olive oil
Pinch of sea salt
Few gratings of Pecorino
Small green chilli, roughly chopped and
    deseeded to your taste
```

Add the ingredients to a blender and blitz well, tasting and adding greater quanitites as you see fit. Best to reserve the chilli seeds as you cut them in case you want to put some back in. This should have a little kick!

Butterbean and Rosemary Hummus
This is Ellie's all-time favourite. Perfect for any season and so easy we can't believe it hasn't been done before. We find we always have ingredients for this at home so whatever's lacking in the kitchen you can at least rustle up some supper out of this quick list.

```
Long sprig of rosemary, stalk removed
400g tin butter beans, drained
3 tablespoons tahini paste
Juice and zest of ½ a lemon, plus extra
    zest to serve
Good glug of best olive oil
Good pinch of sea salt and grinding of
    mixed peppercorns
```

Pound the rosemary leaves with a pestle and mortar. It's important not to skip this bit as this will release the oils from the herb. Add to a blender or food processor with the other ingredients and blitz to form a smooth, cake batter-like mix. Taste and adjust the quantities to suit – it will take a fair amount of oil, lemon juice, tahini and seasoning to pull all the flavours out of this one but when it gets there, it gets it! Spread onto a plate and finish with a drizzle of oil and more lemon zest.

Borlotti with Feta and Olives
Fresh borlotti beans are the glamour pusses of the vegetable patch – and don't they know it. They're not all that easy to come by but if you see them, snap them up quick. Opening a tin of them is absolutely fine, and though you'll miss out on their beautiful pink marbled skins (which you'll find hard to throw away), you will cut out the boiling time.

```
300—400g fresh borlotti beans, shelled
    or 400g tin, drained
1 garlic clove, peeled (if using fresh beans)
100g mixed marinaded olives, stoned and
    roughly chopped
100g feta
Handful of fresh flat leaf parsley, roughly
    chopped
Handful of fresh coriander
Squeeze of lemon juice
Olive oil, for serving
```

If using fresh beans, boil them with a clove of peeled garlic and a little olive oil and salt until tender. Drain and refresh. Otherwise, add the tin to a bowl along with the olives, feta and herbs. Finish with lemon juice and oil and serve.

Sour Cream, Spring Onion and Garlic Dip
Sour cream is dangerously good in a dip. Whether accompanying a hot chilli in the cooler months or as part of a summer mezze, just throw in something from the onion family and a good pinch of seasoning and you're away.

```
100g sour cream
1 spring onion, finely chopped
  (including the green tops)
1 garlic clove, crushed
Small handful of chives, finely chopped
Small squeeze of lemon
Salt and pepper
```

Combine everything together in a bowl and top with some of the chopped chives and an extra grind of black pepper.

If you can't stand the heat, get out of the kitchen — *Gazpacho*

A batch of sweet, tangy gazpacho is a sure-fire way to keep your cool on a midsummer's day. Thick with ripe tomatoes, peppers and cucumber, and given a kick with wafts of raw garlic and fresh chilli, it's one hell of a smooth way to chill out when the kitchen ain't the place to be. Serve in chilled glasses. This recipe serves as many as you like – just put the soup into small glasses if you're feeding lots! It's obvious but the better your tomatoes, the better your gazpacho.

Serves 4, or more in small glasses

Large hunk of stale bread (or fresh is fine, pitta also works)
Ripe tomatoes — 6 large beef, a generous handful of vine, a big handful of baby cherries
1 medium cucumber, peeled, seeded, and roughly chopped
1 red pepper, seeded and roughly sliced
Long glug of best olive oil
½ red chilli, sliced and deseeded to taste
2 garlic cloves, finely sliced
Handful of basil, plus extra to serve
Glug of balsamic vinegar
Salt and pepper

Break up the bread and soak in a small bowl of water. Roughly chop the tomatoes and add to a blender jug, along with the cucumber and red pepper. Slosh in a generous glug of olive oil, the red chilli, garlic and a good pinch of sea salt and grind of pepper. Blend. Throw in a handful of basil leaves, a glug of balsamic vinegar and the soaked bread and blend again. Season appropriately. Chill for a few hours in the fridge – no need to sieve – and serve with a drizzle of olive oil and torn basil.

A cool summer supper for two empty tummies
— *Orecchiette with Anchovies, Baby Tomatoes and Basil*

It's not always true that the sun limits your appetite. Though most of the season is good for grazing, cool evenings and off days call for bigger fillers. We end up stirring together plenty of quick and fresh bowls of pasta that don't rely on the hot and sturdy sauces used later in the year. A pasta salad needn't be the fusili, tinned tuna, grated carrot and sweetcorn often seen on school 'salad carts', either. Halved tomatoes, fine-chopped anchovies and fresh herbs all go quickly onto the plate on a warm evening, and using a different pasta shape to get your mouth around – and cradle – the ingredients livens up a cupboard staple. Inspired by Nigel Slater's Orecchiette with Roast Tomato and Basil Sauce, this recipe is stripped back to let the sweet, ripe juice of the raw baby Santini tomatoes marry well with garlic, anchovies and a hint of dried chilli. If you can get fresh anchovies or *boquerones*, then do – their beautiful silver colour will thread through the dish.

Serves 2

Large handful baby Santini or baby plum tomatoes
3 anchovies from a jar, drained of oil
Glug of good olive oil
Generous pinch of dried chilli flakes
Small handful of fresh basil leaves,
  plus extra for serving
200g dried orecchiette
Good splash of single cream
Pepper

Halve the tomatoes lengthways and put into 2 serving bowls with their juices. Finely chop the anchovies and add to the bowls, along with a couple of twists of black pepper, a glug of best olive oil and the chilli flakes. Tear in the basil and turn the ingredients to combine.

Bring a pan of salted water to a rolling boil. Add the pasta and cook according to the packet instructions until al dente. Drain, reserving about a tablespoon of the water. Add the tomato and anchovy mixture to the pan and return to the lowest heat. Turn gently and add a splash of cream, letting the beads of oil and cream remain separate. Turn back into the serving bowl and serve with extra basil and a little pepper. Parmesan, capers and garlic are all lovely additions.

A pair of summer chickens
— *Chicken with Yogurt and Capers*
— *Coronation or Royal Wedding Chicken*

We all know about spring chickens but what about summer ones? They're good too. Whatever the season, we tend to go for 'outdoorsy types' when it comes to our birds. If you can afford to go free range or organic, you'll have a much tastier and guilt-free lunch. Poaching chicken breasts doesn't look very pretty but it's a healthy and light way of cooking that keeps the chicken moist and ideal for shredding into salads. As a friend taught us, the finer you shred the chicken, the tastier the salad and clean fingernails really are the best tools for the job!

Chicken with Yogurt and Capers
Passed down by Rosie's mother-in-law, this recipe is a simple summer classic, perfect with a crisp green salad and some crusty bread to mop up the dressing.

Serves 2

```
2 skinless chicken breasts, halved lengthways
Pinch of salt
Splash of white wine vinegar
1 bay leaf
8 tablespoons natural yogurt
2 tablespoons mayonnaise
3 tablespoons capers, rinsed
3-4 rosemary springs, finely chopped
Handful of fresh mint, finely chopped
Salad leaves and lemon wedges, to serve
```

Place the chicken into a wide, shallow pan or a lidded frying pan and barely cover with water. Add the salt, vinegar and bay leaf and turn on the heat. Once the water is boiling vigorously, turn each piece of chicken over and remove the pan from the heat. Cover and let it rest for 15 minutes until the chicken is thoroughly cooked and no pink remains.

Meanwhile, combine the other ingredients in a bowl, saving some mint for later. When cool enough to handle, shred the chicken into the bowl, mix and serve with the remaining mint. A few salad leaves of your choice and a lemon wedge wouldn't go amiss either.

Coronation or Royal Wedding Chicken

We love curry powder and we're not ashamed. If you're going to use it, don't be shy, pile it onto soft onions ready for your kedgeree and crown that Coronation Chicken with heaps of the stuff. Despite its school-dinner reputation, curry powder gives a wonderful background warmth to Anglo-Indian dishes punctuated by delicious pops of sweetness from juicy sultanas and crunch from toasted almonds. We've added some mango here too to make perhaps the ultimate picnic dish fit for kings, queens and plebeians alike. Serve with crispy lettuce and cold white wine or, better still, chilled sparkling wine.

Serves 4

```
2 large chicken breasts
Pinch of salt
2 bay leaves
Thumb-sized piece of fresh ginger,
  peeled and grated
Cinnamon stick
Handful of peppercorns
50g sultanas
50g flaked almonds
1 tablespoon coriander seeds
2 heaped tablespoons curry powder
4 tablespoons Greek yogurt
4 tablespoons mayonnaise
Flesh of a small mango, finely diced
Handful of fresh coriander, finely chopped
Salt and pepper
```

Put the chicken in a pan with the salt, bay leaves, ginger, cinnamon stick and peppercorns and poach as on page 66.

Soak the sultanas in warm water to plump-up and toast the flaked almonds and coriander seeds in a dry frying pan.

Combine the curry powder with the yogurt and mayonnaise in a bowl. Shred the chicken as finely as possible and add to the bowl. Stir to combine. Add the drained sultanas, toasted almonds and coriander seeds. Stir again. Finally add the mango, fresh coriander and some seasoning, stir once more and serve.

A cool and reviving salad when the fridge is bare
— *Cucumber and Carrot Salad with Sesame and Chilli*

It can be hard to shop when the weather is unpredictable, nor is it an attractive chore when the sun is beating down. This rather sad state of affairs, as far as the fridge is concerned, means that necessity and desperation are the mother of invention when it comes to feeding yourself. If your storecupboard is well-stocked, then all you need here are the ingredients offered up by the salad drawer or garden at this time of year: a little cucumber, a carrot, a sprig of mint and a solitary lime. Fresh red chillies are ideal (keep them in the freezer if you can't get through them quickly enough), though a pinch of dried flakes would do fine. We chop and change the way we eat this – grate your vegetables if you want a less elegant salad or slice them into fine ribbons with a vegetable peeler. For some reason we find there's more flavour in the latter. If you have any unsalted peanuts knocking around, crush and sprinkle some on top for a bit of luxury.

Serves 1

For the salad
½ cucumber
1 medium carrot
½ small red chilli, deseeded to taste
Handful of sesame seeds, toasted
Handful of mint leaves, torn
Handful of coriander leaves, torn
Handful of unsalted peanuts (optional)

For the dressing
Juice of 1 lime
Glug of sesame oil
Glug of fish sauce
Dash of soy sauce

Peel the vegetables if you wish, and coarsely grate or peel into thin ribbons directly into your serving bowl. Add the chilli, sesame, herbs and peanuts if using them.

Mix all the dressing ingredients in a cup and turn with the carrot and cucumber. Serve immediately.

Two lovely summer salads
— *Radicchio, Pear and Gorgonzola*
— *Prosciutto, Melon and Spinach*

These classic salads need little in the way of introduction or preparation. Both rely on three key ingredients which, when thrown together by even the clumsiest of hands, make delicious summer salads you can't help but revisit with your fork again and again.

Radicchio, Pear and Gorgonzola
Bitter but beautiful radicchio looks so good in the summer sun – its veined, bright purple leaves giving the perfect amount of bite to complement juicy slices of pear, chunks of creamy Gorgonzola and a drizzle of fragrant honey and mustard dressing. Pecans make a lovely addition here if you want some extra crunch.

1 head of radicchio, divided into leaves
  and washed and dried
2 ripe pears, peeled and sliced
200g Gorgonzola

For the dressing
6 tablespoons olive oil
1 teaspoon balsamic vinegar
1 teaspoon white wine vinegar
1 teaspoon clear honey
1 teaspoon Dijon mustard
Pinch of salt

Spread the leaves over a large plate. Put the dressing ingredients into a jam jar and shake to mix then pour a little dressing over the leaves. Toss the leaves until lightly coated then spread them out again. Top with the pear and large chunks of Gorgonzola, drizzle over a little more dressing and serve.

Prosciutto, Melon and Spinach

Try to find the ripest melon in the bunch for this salad.
When you're choosing your fruit, look at the round section
where the vine was once attached and have a good prod and
a sniff – it should be soft and fragrant. This salad is the
essence of an Italian summer.

    1 ripe melon, sliced into wedges
    85g prosciutto
    Handful of baby spinach
    Juice of ½ a lemon
    Pepper

Lay the melon wedges on a plate and loosely lay the ham
slices over and around them. Scatter over the baby spinach,
drizzle with lemon juice and grind over a little pepper.

Get some heat
— Summer's Biggest and Best Barbecue

You can never fake the smokiness and dark charred sweetness of meat cooked over coals, so while the weather's good, get yourself outside, burn your fingers and make a mess. It's not just meat that gets the flame-grilled treatment here – peppers, courgettes and the aubergines for Ellie's baba ghanoush (see page 78) are all blackened over flaming coals for optimum smokiness and flavour. Our old faithful butter-free corn on the cob is even better for the cobs being cooked over coal until their husks blacken and start floating away like bits of burnt newspaper. Show your meat some love with a few simple marinades and accompaniments and get your cook on, Salad Club style.

Handed down to Rosie by Chilean *Asado* (barbecue) maestros and shared here for the first time, read on for some tips on how to do it, South-American style.

Ditch the light bags and charcoal briquettes. One's barbecue ambitions are usually fulfilled at the weekend when you should have time to light the barbecue at least an hour or so before you're ready to cook. If you do, go for a bag of proper lump charcoal, which will burn hotter for longer, giving you enough time to cook up a second helping for any stragglers. It also produces far less ash and smoke that can make things a little anti-social.

No need for fire lighters with the broadsheet tunnel of fire. A genius and fail-safe way to light a barbecue without firelighters or paraffin. Every fire-starter worth his salt in Chile would open the ceremony with this trick.

You will need
1 old broadsheet newspaper
1 empty wine bottle
Matches/lighter

- Roll up individual newspaper pages (long end to long end at a slight diagonal) until you have a long tube of newspaper.
- Wrap each tube around the wine bottle and carefully tie a knot.
- Repeat until the wide part of the bottle is wrapped in about 6–8 tubes of paper but keep the neck of the bottle free.
- Place the bottle in the centre of the barbecue and tip your coals around it, making sure there are plenty of coals pushed up to the sides of the bottle.

- Holding the top of the bottle, slowly pull it out of the paper tunnel leaving a hole where it once was.
- Light the edges of the paper knots and leave the tunnel to do its work. The air in the tunnel will fuel the flames and help the coals to catch. Push some of the coals closer to the flames if need be.

Oil and season the grill. To make sure nothing sticks to the grill and to add a touch more flavour, cut an onion in half, skewer the closed end with a fork, dip into seasoned vegetable or groundnut oil and rub over the grill between each course.

Know when to season and rest your meat. By all means pepper, but don't salt your meat before it hits the grill. Wait until you turn it, then throw over a generous amount of sea salt and repeat when you turn it the second time. That way the salt works its way into the meat rather than drawing the moisture out. Annoy your impatient guests and give meat time to rest before serving, just as you would in the kitchen.

On the grill
— *Tagliata con Rucola*
— *Mango Salsa*

Tagliata con Rucola

This Italian classic is the king of all 'man salads'. Strips of perfectly charred, rare steak lounging casually on a bed of rocket topped with shavings of Parmesan. Washed down with a light red on a summer's night, this never fails to satisfy those macho, carnivorous cravings for bloody, salty meat. Be sure to get the best quality ingredients and they'll do most of the work for you. Oh, and don't worry if it's not quite barbecue weather, a smoking hot griddle pan does justice. Rocket is so easy to grow in pots or beds. Sow seeds all through late spring and summer for a constant supply of peppery goodness. Be sure to pick it regularly as it likes to bolt and flower when you're not paying attention.

Serves 6

800g rib eye or sirloin steak
Glug of olive oil
150g wild rocket
100g Parmesan
Olive oil and balsamic vinegar, to serve
Salt and pepper

This method is for rare steak (it shouldn't be any other way, really). Remove the meat from the fridge at least an hour before cooking (if possible) and rub all over with olive oil and pepper. When the coals are white (or your griddle pan is smoking hot), it's time to cook. Throw the steaks onto the grill and push them down all over with the back of some tongs. After 2 minutes turn each steak and throw over a few large pinches of uncrushed sea salt.

After another 2 minutes, throw over another pinch of salt and remove the steaks to a chopping board – preferably one with a ridge to catch the juices – and leave to rest for 5 minutes. Pile the rocket on a large plate, slice the steaks into roughly 1cm wide slices and scatter over the rocket.

Shave over the Parmesan and drizzle with a little olive oil and a splash of balsamic vinegar.

Mango Salsa

Mango, with its thick flesh and fragrant juices, is a great partner for the welcome heft of well-chargrilled red meat.

```
1 mango, peeled and diced*
1 small green chilli, finely chopped
  and deseeded to taste
Juice of 1 lime
¼ small red onion, very finely sliced
Handful of fresh mint leaves, finely chopped
Pepper
```

Combine the ingredients in a bright bowl, cover with clingfilm and refrigerate until needed – about 30 minutes is ideal.

*The easiest way to peel and dice a mango is to lay it on a chopping board and take a small but sharp knife to either side of the length of the stone. You should come away with two clean lengths, the flesh of which you can score a criss-cross pattern into, close down to the skin. Flip the flesh inside out to create a hedgehog, then slice out the chunks in one go. Do it over a bowl to reserve the juices. Return to the stone and stand it upright to slice off any extra flesh.

More on the grill
— *Chilli and Lime Corn on the Cob*
— *Chargrilled Peppers and Courgettes with Basil and Garlic Oil*

Chilli and Lime Corn on the Cob

Toothpicks at the ready for this barbecue stalwart and childhood favourite. We know it's summer when we see the first cobs on the market, tightly swaddled in their husks, unkempt hair poking out, some peeling back their collars to reveal perfect lines of plump yellow corn crying out for the barbecue treatment. Make sure you keep the husks on as they make perfect smoking jackets!

Serves 6

```
6 corn cobs in their husks or wrapped in foil
2 limes
Handful of chilli flakes
Salt and pepper
```

When the coals are white-hot, place the corn on the grill and cook for about 20–25 minutes, turning occasionally, until the husks are black. Carefully remove the husks, squeeze over the lime juice, sprinkle the chilli flakes, season and serve. 'BUTTER!', we hear you cry… Not this time. We find summer corn so naturally creamy and sweet that it honestly doesn't need any butter. In fact we've served these up to people who were convinced we'd buttered them up.

Chargrilled Peppers and Courgettes with Basil and Garlic Oil

Courgettes and peppers can be a pair of tasteless dullards if left to their own devices. Peppers are only really worth bothering with if they've been burnt to a crisp on the outside, steaming the flesh within until deliciously soft, silky and smoky. Green peppers, however, are beyond help. Courgettes need a shorter, vicious grilling until branded with griddle marks and just starting to soften. Serve both with a drizzle of basil-and-garlic-infused oil and they won't let you down.

Serves 6

```
3 sweet red peppers
3–4 small courgettes, sliced in half or
   in thirds lengthways
4 tablespoons extra virgin olive oil
   (plus a little extra for coating the
   courgettes)
Bunch of basil leaves
3 garlic cloves
Squeeze of lemon
Salt and pepper
```

When the flames are still gently licking the grill, throw on the peppers and leave them to blacken all over, turning once or twice. Once the flames have died down, season the grill and coat the courgette slices with olive oil and a little salt. Barbecue the slices until they're scored with deep black griddle marks and starting to soften (about 3 minutes each side).

Blitz the basil, garlic, oil and lemon in a food processor to a smooth paste and season. Loosen with more lemon juice if required. Peel and slice the peppers and lay the slices on a board or plate with the griddled courgettes. Drizzle with the basil oil and serve.

Supper for when the air starts to cool
— *Lamb Cutlets with Warm, Creamy Flageolet Beans and Baba Ghanoush*

The title says it all, really. One of those recipes that does exactly what it says on the tin!

Serves 4

For the lamb
8 lamb cutlets
Juice of ½ a lemon
Dash of olive oil
2 sprigs of thyme
2 sprigs of rosemary
Pepper

To serve
100g feta, crumbled
1 tablespoon Greek yogurt
Squeeze of lemon
Pinch of sumac
Sprig of thyme

For the baba ghanoush
1 large aubergine
2 tablespoons tahini
Juice of ½ a lemon
½ garlic clove, crushed
Handful of sesame seeds
Handful of fresh parsley, roughly chopped
Dash of olive oil
Salt and pepper

For the beans
150g diced pancetta (optional)
1 tin flageolet beans, drained
1 garlic clove, minced
2 tablespoons crème fraîche
2 sprigs of rosemary
Salt and pepper

Marinate the lamb in the lemon juice, oil, pepper, thyme and rosemary and cover with clingfilm. Refrigerate for an hour. Combine the feta, yogurt and lemon juice in a small bowl and top with sumac and thyme. Refrigerate.

Turn the grill high and make the baba ghanoush. Pierce the aubergine and grill on all sides to blacken the skin – this is essential for creating a smoky flavour. Keep the grill on. Allow to cool in a colander set in the sink and, when cool enough to handle, peel and discard the skin. Mash the flesh with a fork to remove excess water and transfer to a bowl. Combine vigorously with the tahini, lemon juice, garlic and seasoning. Just before serving, toast the sesame seeds and scatter on top, with a generous handful of parsley and a little olive oil. (Try it also with toasted pine nuts and coriander or walnuts and beads of pomegranate.)

Empty the flageolet into a small pan and warm through with the other ingredients, loosening with a drip of oil if necessary. This dish is extra good if you start the pan off by browning pancetta in it. Meanwhile, place the lamb cutlets under the grill and keep an eye on them – if they're very small they'll be ready after a few minutes on each side. Serve everything as soon as the lamb is browned.

Playing with pizzettas
— *Pizza Base*
— *Salad Club's Marinara Sauce*
— *Pizza Marinara*

Pizza Base

We have to be honest and admit defeat in the pizza dough department. We simply couldn't come up with anything to beat this recipe, adapted from one by Jamie Oliver.

```
Makes 6—8 medium pizzas

2 x 7g sachets of instant yeast
1 tablespoon caster sugar
4 tablespoons olive oil
650ml water at room temperature
1kg strong white bread flour, plus extra
    for dusting
1 level tablespoon salt
```

Mix the yeast, sugar, olive oil and water together and set aside. Sift the flour and salt into a large bowl. Make a well in the centre and pour in the yeast mixture. Gradually bring the mixture together using a fork or a wooden spoon until all of the flour is incorporated. Turn the dough onto a floured work surface and knead until you have a smooth, springy dough.

Lightly dust the bowl with flour and return the dough to it. Sprinkle a little flour over the top of the dough and cover the bowl with a damp tea towel. Leave the dough to rise in warm room for about an hour until it has doubled in size.

Briefly knead the dough on a floured work surface, divide the dough into balls and either roll-out and use immediately or wrap in clingfilm and store in the fridge or freezer until needed.

Salad Club's Marinara Sauce

Whether you've successfully harvested a glut of tomatoes or snapped up a bunch at the shops, one of the best ways to prolong that wonderful greenhouse scent and flavour into autumn is to make up a big batch of marinara sauce.

```
Makes about 1 litre

8 garlic cloves, peeled and crushed
Handful of fresh marjoram leaves
Handful of fresh basil leaves
8 tablespoons quality extra virgin olive oil
3kg ripe tomatoes, blanched, peeled and
    roughly chopped
1 or 2 Parmesan rinds
Salt and pepper
```

Heat the garlic and herbs in the olive oil over a low heat for 4–5 minutes until soft but not taking on any colour. Add the tomatoes and Parmesan rind, bring to the boil, season well and simmer gently for 30–40 minutes until thick enough to spread*. Check for seasoning and adjust to taste. Push the sauce through a sieve into jars, freezer bags or straight into a bowl ready to spread over your pizzettas. Make sure you scrape all the sticky tomato goodness from the bottom of the sieve. The sauce should keep for a week in the fridge and you can freeze individual portions until you need them.

Pizza Marinara

A classic Italian, cheese-free pizza, covered in garlic and dried oregano. Make the base as thin as you can for this one and be generous with the Marinara Sauce.

```
Pizza base (roughly 20cm diameter and
    rolled thinly)
2 tablespoons Marinara Sauce
3 garlic cloves, crushed
1 teaspoon dried oregano
Extra virgin olive oil
```

Fire up the oven to its maximum temperature. Spread the sauce over the pizza base. Crush over half of the garlic and sprinkle on the oregano. Drizzle with olive oil and bake for 8–10 minutes until just crisp at the edges.

Remove from the oven, top with the remaining garlic and a second drizzle of olive oil.

Pizza Toppings

We're not going to tell you what to put on your pizza – have fun using up what's in your fridge or store cupboard. Here are a few combinations we like:

```
Anchovies, courgette, mozzarella, cherry
tomatoes and capers (finished off with some
fresh parsley).

Gorgonzola, radicchio, sage and pear.

Sunblushed tomatoes and ricotta (with some
rosemary pushed into the dough).

Potato (boiled and sliced thinly), Parma ham,
Dolcelatte and thyme.
```

Some summer comfort
— *Courgette, Sage and Parmesan Risotto*

While our carb cravings are somewhat curbed in the summer months, there's still the odd night when all that will satisfy is a steaming plate of rice. More often than not, these cravings rear their ugly heads during a storm or a sudden drop in temperature that scares us back into our jumpers and has us scrabbling around for our heavy pots and pans. There's no shame in stuffing your face occasionally in the summer, just make sure you've got plenty of people over to stop you polishing it all off yourself (and to bring the wine).

Serves 8

1 litre vegetable or chicken stock
3 tablespoons olive oil
1 large white onion, finely chopped
3 garlic cloves, finely chopped
2 sticks celery, finely chopped
20 sage leaves
600g Carnaroli or Arborio rice
Large glass of white wine
3 small or 2 medium courgettes
50g butter
70g Parmesan, grated
Salt and pepper

To serve
Lemon wedges
Parmesan for grating

Heat the stock in a pan over a low heat with a ladle at the ready. Meanwhile heat the olive oil in a wide, shallow pan and throw in the onions, garlic and celery. Turn the heat right down and fry for about 15 minutes, stirring every now and then.

Finely chop half of the sage leaves and add them to the pan along with the rice. Keep everything moving around the pan until the rice is coated with oil and slightly translucent. Add the wine and turn up the heat.

Once the wine has reduced, season well and add a ladle of stock. Simmer over a low heat and stir until the stock has been absorbed. Keep adding stock by the ladleful and letting it absorb into the rice while you stir.

In our experience, risotto can take as little as 20 minutes or as long as an hour to cook! Always have some spare stock or boiling water ready in case you have a particularly resistant batch of rice. It seems that whenever we try making risotto in a hurry, the rice refuses to 'turn' and become soft, so don't rush. Now the bottle's open, pour yourself a glass of wine, gather people around the hob and take turns with ladling and stirring.

Once the rice is soft but still retains some bite, slice the courgettes into the pan in thin ribbons with a potato peeler and stir. Add the butter and Parmesan, cover the pan and remove from the heat. Leave for 3 minutes until beautifully creamy then take to the table to serve with lemon wedges and extra Parmesan.

Sage crisps
Melt a small knob of butter in a pan until gently bubbling then add the remaining sage leaves. When crisp, remove to a sheet of kitchen paper to drain. Top each plate of risotto with a few sage crisps for added crunch and intense sageness.

A brisk dip in the freezer
— *Fresh Berry Ices*

Though you can happily part-exchange some of the fresh
berries here for frozen, there's little point if you can go fresh
all the way – this is a collection of summer's best fruits so
they should be affordable and at their most flavoursome.
You could simmer any leftover berries with a little sugar
and elderflower cordial, water or liqueur to make a quick
coulis then refrigerate before spooning over the ices. This
recipe is easy and cheap enough that you could make up a
few different flavours to store in the freezer for unexpected
hot days – elderflower with a hint of orange blossom or
cucumber and mint, perhaps.

Serves 4

275g fresh summer berries (we used a mix of
   blueberries, blackberries and raspberries)
½ glass of cold, dry white wine (Pinot Grigio
   is a good bet)
Juice and zest of 1 lime
1 tablespoon caster sugar

Put all the ingredients into a blender or food processor and
blitz quickly to coarsely pulverise the fruit. Pour into a small
plastic or freezer-proof container and freeze. Every 2 hours
fork-up the mixture to break up the ice granules. Continue
freezing and forking until set. Serve in glasses. If you want
to freeze the mix really quickly, pour into ice cube trays for
smaller portions, cutting out the forking stage, or freeze in
pre-prepared ice lolly moulds.

A pudding for a rosy-shadowed evening
— Grilled Peaches in Wine

This is a variant of a classic Italian pudding copied worldwide for its timeless style and easy summer appeal. Unlike *îles flottantes* or tiramisu, it isn't lodged in our memories of our parents' 1980s dinner parties but does, of course, rely on perfectly ripe fruit that should be selected with care. Use chilled dry white wine without exception and a decent pudding wine if you have some. You could also try this with nectarines or fresh apricots.

Serves 8

```
8 ripe peaches
1 vanilla pod
½ glass of dry white wine, chilled
½ glass of dessert wine
Juice of ½ a lemon
1 tablespoon caster or light brown sugar
Mascarpone, for serving
```

Halve and stone the peaches and lay them cut side down in a roasting tin. Split the vanilla pod and add to the tin with both wines and the lemon juice. Agitate the vanilla pod a little, then cover with clingfilm and refrigerate for an hour or two. Heat the grill to medium, turn the peach halves cut side up and sprinkle with the sugar. Grill for 5–10 minutes until charred golden brown. Serve in small bowls with the juices and a dollop of mascarpone.

Tip: An easy summer pudding can be made on the barbecue when the coals are too cool for cooking meat but still retain a good amount of heat – it seems a waste to light it only to use it for steaks and burgers. Place a few summer fruits – berries and stoned fruits are particularly good – in the centre of a large piece of aluminium foil. Bring the sides up to form a pouch and add a splash of wine, liqueur or cordial and a little vanilla sugar, then wrap tightly at the top and add to the grill. Check on your parcel every 15 minutes as it steams. A chopped banana with squares of dark chocolate makes for another good parcel.

Much ado about chocolate
— *Chocolate Espresso Mousse*

I think most of us would enjoy rounding off a meal with a small cup of rich *mousse au chocolat* and a coffee. Or, even better, both at the same time. There's a tendency to be hysterical and girly when it comes to chocolate – with words such as 'indulge', 'treat' and 'bliss' being bandied around at the mere mention of the stuff. Well, we refuse to get involved with all that nonsense. Men, women and children like chocolate. Chocolate is good. That is all.

Enough for 8 espresso-sized cups

```
1 double espresso
200g good-quality dark chocolate (plus extra
    to serve)
3 free range egg whites
Drop of lemon juice
100g caster sugar
250ml double cream
1 free range egg yolk
```

Make a strong double espresso and leave it to cool. Break the chocolate into pieces and melt gently in a heatproof bowl over a pan of simmering water (making sure the bottom of the bowl doesn't touch the water).

Put the egg whites in a large bowl with a drop of lemon juice and whisk until stiff peaks form, gradually adding the sugar as you go. In another bowl (sorry about the washing up) lightly whip the cream until it forms gentle mounds – you don't want it to be too thick.

Once the chocolate has melted, stir in the coffee and let it cool before stirring in the egg yolk. Gently fold in the cream and finally the egg whites with a metal spoon.

Refrigerate for 30 minutes and serve with shavings of dark chocolate.

The perfect cake for a lazy summer afternoon
— *Honey, Almond and Polenta Cake*

Have you ever noticed that whenever you make a cake, those eating it just can't resist commenting on the moisture levels. If people aren't silently nodding and mumbling 'mmmm, that's moist' from the side of their cake holes, while catching falling crumbs in their palms, chances are you've baked a dry one and should be ashamed of yourself! This easy recipe always scores well on the moisture scale and should be washed down with cup after cup of refreshing Earl Grey tea on a lazy summer afternoon.

Serves 8–10

225g unsalted butter
225g golden caster sugar
4 large free range eggs
30g self-raising flour
35g fine polenta
200g ground almonds
1 teaspoon baking powder
Pinch of salt
3 tablespoons clear honey
Zest of 2 lemons
Handful of whole blanched almonds,
   to decorate

Preheat the oven to 180°C/gas mark 4. Butter and line a 20cm cake tin. Cream the butter and sugar until light and fluffy then add the eggs, one at a time. Sift the flour, polenta, ground almonds and baking powder with a pinch of salt and add to the mix. Stir in the honey and lemon zest and transfer to the cake tin.

Lightly push the whole almonds into the mixture in any pattern that takes your fancy. Bake on the middle shelf of the oven for 1 hour or until a knife or skewer inserted into the centre comes out clean. Remove from the oven and leave to cool in the tin. Run a knife around the edge, transfer to a plate and serve with Greek yogurt or crème fraîche and a big pot of tea.

Autumn

Autumn

With our clunky pots and pans back on the hob, and the short-lived summer light beginning to fade, it's time to get back to our kitchens and resume normal service for the rest of the year. It's with a heavy heart that we bid goodbye to summer's spontaneity, salads and barbecues but we welcome autumn's soups, stews and curries like long lost friends. Let's commit summer's al fresco meals to memory and get back to the business of huddling around the table for warmth.

As the darker nights and colder fingers start to set in, the colours of the turning leaves and low shafts of sunlight find their way into the cooking pot with autumn's harvest. Our kitchen tables take on a rustic and earthy charm – replete with plates of tender meat, sturdy pulses, sweet roots and punchy spices – the type of food that imparts warmth to the often bright but shortening, chilly days. As our ovens whirr back into life, the pace at the kitchen table slows down and we take pleasure once again in the process of cooking from scratch and letting things brew. The pages of our notebooks become increasingly splattered this season as the ladles and wooden spoons come out in force and the kitchen starts to feel properly lived in again.

While our kitchens are increasingly busy, so too are we. This autumn, in particular, has been an epic one for us. Along with testing, tweaking and writing these recipes, we embarked on a whirlwind tour of the country with our street food stall and building work commenced on our very first restaurant, French & Grace. Like gearing up for the start of a new school term, we're full of nerves and excitement as we prepare to open our doors around the time this book goes to print.

A Menu for Autumn

Breakfast & Brunch

...

Crunchy Granola
Creamed Corn with Crispy Bacon on Sourdough
Harissa-baked Beans with Chorizo, Eggs and Feta

Something to Relish

...

Red Onion Marmalade
Spiced Plum Chutney
Tomato Chilli Jam

Bowl Food

...

Pumpkin and Ginger Soup
Tomato, Herb and Sourdough Soup
Smoked Haddock, King Prawn and Sweet Potato Chowder
Wasabi Beef Ramen

Suppertime

...

Sweet Pumpkin Curry, Coconut Okra and Quick Chapati
Fillet of Jerk Salmon
One Pot Chicken Cooked with Bacon, Potatoes, Mushrooms and
Tarragon and Fresh Watercress Salad
Lamb, Squash and Orzo Stew with Minted Yogurt
Aubergine Stuffed with Ground Lamb
Sausages with Braised Puy Lentils, Potatoes and Crème Fraîche
Lamb Kabab Cooked with Cherries
Smoked Paprika Pork Chops with Celeriac and Squash Rösti
Parppadelle with Duck Ragu
Warm Barley and Almond Tabbouleh with Pomegranate
Pear and Goats' Cheese Tarts

Teatime Puds

...

Chocolate Orange Beetroot Brownies
Lemon, Yogurt and Blackberry Muffins
Spiced Banana Bread
Apricot, Pistachio and Almond Flapjacks
Plum and Ginger Crumble
Flourless Chocolate, Prune and Brandy Cake

Bowls of cupboard love
— *Crunchy Granola*

A far cry from the boxes of dry and flavourless breakfast cereals found at the supermarket, this recipe for rich baked oats and nuts packs more spice than any shop-bought granola. Substituting big brands with a bowl of this every other day transforms breakfast into a bit of a luxury event, turning the milk deliciously sweet and spicey. There's something satisfying to be had from the tinkling noise of these toasted clusters hitting the bowl in the morning. It's also good eaten dry, in handfuls, or with a yogurt and fruit compote, and the smell of it baking on a wet Sunday morning is deeply rewarding. We adapted this recipe from Molly Wizenberg's adaptation of Nigella Lawson's recipe. It yields exactly one large kilner jar, which can be stored in the fridge or cupboard.

For the main mix
700g jumbo rolled oats
150g raw almonds
100g pecan halves, broken with a rolling pin
100g sunflower seeds
100g sesame seeds*
100g light brown sugar**
2 good teaspoons ground cinnamon
1 good teaspoon ground ginger
Large pinch sea salt

For the coating
100ml maple syrup
2 tablespoons clear honey
1 good teaspoon vanilla extract
2 teaspoon vegetable oil
200ml apple juice

Preheat the oven to 190°C/gas mark 5. Add the main mix ingredients to a large bowl. In a separate bowl, mix together the coating ingredients. Mix both bowls separately and add the wet bowl mix to the dry, stirring well to combine. Spread evenly onto two lined baking trays and bake for 30–40 minutes until golden, stirring and turning the mixture every 10 minutes or so. This will give an even colour to the granola and help to keep it from sticking to the tray. Remove from the oven and stir well to stop it from drying into a hard sheet. Set aside to cool and crisp up, then transfer to a sealable jar and let the addiction begin!

* Or use up any nuts from your cupboard. I finished off the ends of pine nut and hazlenut packets which worked really well. Just add what you like.

** I actually mixed my sugars a bit – third white, third light brown and third muscovado – because they were knocking around the cupboard and the darkest sugar seems to make a great fit. Obviously this is breakfast, so feel free to lessen the sugars if you like.

Breakfast American-style
— Creamed Corn with Crispy Grilled Bacon on Sourdough

There's something typically North American about creamed corn. Our imaginations leads us to believe that people who live in clapboard houses eat it fresh from the plantation in rocking chairs positioned on the porch, under blazing, brilliant skies.

Corn's natural creaminess won't be found in tins so be sure to buy fresh cobs at a market if possible, as they'll be far cheaper than the plastic-wrapped stuff. It can be hard to hold back from eating the kernels raw once you've cut them free and we recently found ourselves just scoffing at it like fruit before plunging into water. The creamed corn itself can be made as partner to a hot stew or braised chicken thighs, but with a dash of cream and a grating of nutmeg, we find it is best friends of all with salty, crisped bacon and chewy, toasted bread. Wash down with a glass of freshly-squeezed orange juice and a strong coffee at the weekend.

Serves 2

```
1 small white onion, very finely chopped
2 knobs of butter, plus extra for spreading
2 corn cobs, de-robed
¾ cup water
6 rashers of smoked streaky bacon
Glug of single cream
Freshly grated nutmeg, to taste
2 thick slices sourdough bread
Salt and pepper
```

Preheat the grill to medium-high. Sweat the onion in a pan on a low heat in a knob of butter. Stand the corn vertically in a large bowl and use a long, sharp knife to cut away the kernels. Repeat with a second cob and try to include the base of the kernels, where lots of the juice is held. Add them to the onions, stir and add the water. Add a knob of butter and bring to a simmer under a lid for 10 minutes.

Lay out the bacon on a foil-lined baking tray. Grill on the highest shelf until crisp, turning half way.

When the kernels are tender, add a little glug of cream and grate in a good seasoning of nutmeg, tasting as you go. Season modestly and blitz with a hand blender until smooth. Keep warm while you toast or grill the bread. Butter it lightly, then top with the corn and bacon.

A hearty brunch for another working weekend
— *Harissa Baked Beans with Chorizo, Eggs and Feta*

We're slowly getting used to working at the weekends and giving up our lie-ins but, sometimes, we need some serious fuel to keep us going, especially if we've been burning the candle at both ends. This spicy take on baked beans will get even the most weary of workers up and out before lunchtime and should see them through the afternoon, too.

Serves 4

Olive oil, for cooking
100g spicy cooking chorizo, diced
3 shallots, sliced
2 garlic cloves, sliced
1 teaspoon dried oregano
2 x 400g tins cannellini beans
2 tablespoons harissa (see Ellie's recipe
   on page 148)
400g tin chopped tomatoes
1 tablespoon sugar (or to taste)
1 tablespoon red wine vinegar
4 free range eggs
100g feta
Pinch of sumac (optional)
Sourdough toast, to serve

Preheat the oven to 160°C/gas mark 3. Warm a splash of olive oil in a shallow ovenproof pan and add the chorizo, shallots, garlic and oregano. Fry gently for 5 minutes until the chorizo has released its oil and the shallots are starting to soften. Add the beans (one tin with its water, the other without), harissa, tomatoes, sugar and vinegar. Simmer gently for about 15 minutes until thickened, adding more water if it starts to look too dry.

Make 4 holes in the beans with the back of a wooden spoon and crack an egg into each. Top with the crumbled feta and bake for 8–10 minutes until the eggs are cooked but the yolks still runny. Sprinkle with sumac and serve with sourdough toast and glasses of freshly squeezed orange juice.

Something to relish
— Red Onion Marmalade
— Spiced Plum Chutney
— Tomato Chilli Jam

Red Onion Marmalade

Autumn is the season for brewing, bottling and preserving and it's around this time that we withdraw to the hob to put a jam jar lid on whatever we can pickle in a pot. Red onion marmalade is an easy one to start with, and makes good friends with cheese and biscuits, sticky roasted meats and warm, seasonal salads.

Be sure to add the vinegars at the end of the slow cooking, so as to keep a proper kick in the jar. If you're one for dousing your fish and chips with vinegar and feeling the choking vapour at the back of your mouth, then follow this recipe well. If you're not so keen on the vinegar hit, maybe add them a little earlier and let them evaporate, though note that you will lose some of the sharp flavours that pair well with red onions.

Makes 4 jam-sized jars

2 tablespoons olive oil
6 large red onions, peeled and finely sliced
3-4 whole cloves
200g brown sugar
300ml red or white wine vinegar
50ml balsamic vinegar
Pepper

Heat the olive oil in a heavy-bottomed saucepan over a medium heat and add the onions. Add the cloves and a few grinds of black pepper. Reduce the heat to low, cover the pan and allow to cook very slowly, stirring occasionally. It's vital you don't rush the onions as the slow cooking will caramelise and develop the flavour, as well as reducing the texture to the right consistency. This really should take 30–40 minutes until completely softened and starting to colour.

Add the sugar, turn up the heat to high and stir until dissolved. Remove the lid and stir frequently for 25–30 minutes until the mixture is dark brown and thick. Remove the pan from the heat and cool for a few minutes. Add the vinegars and return to the heat for 10 minutes until gooey. Draw a spoon across the bottom of the pan – it should leave a clear track across the base for a couple of seconds.

Remove from the heat and spoon into sterilised jars, turning upside down once the lid is sealed. Refrigerate once opened.

Spiced Plum Chutney

The plums came early this year. By mid August the tree in Rosie's allotment was sagging under the weight of ripe fruit, their dusty purple jackets nodding on the branches. At around the same time, one of the grocers on the market had a glut to sell before the weekend and gave us a couple of punnets. Too many to eat there and then, so into the frugal pot they go on a rainy autumn day.

Makes 7 medium-sized jars

1.6kg plums, stoned and roughly chopped
375g granulated sugar
350ml balsamic vinegar
150ml white wine vinegar
150ml apple juice
10 whole cloves
10 whole pimento or allspice
1 teaspoon ground cinnamon
1 teaspoon ground nutmeg
1 large white onion, finely diced

Place all the ingredients in a large pan and place on a low heat, stirring to dissolve the sugar. Turn the heat to high and bring to the boil, then reduce the heat to low again. Leave for 1½ to 2 hours or until thickened. Spoon directly into sterilised jars and seal tightly.

Tomato Chilli Jam

This recipe just scrapes its way into autumn as the tomato season draws to a close and we start to look for ways to extend that evocative greenhouse flavour into the colder months. This jam is a great way to use up any tomatoes too ripe for the salad bowl and the natural pectin in the tomato seeds helps the jam to set, so there's no need for any fancy stuff. People tend to get very possessive over their chilli jam if given a jar so if you plan on giving any away, make a nice big batch to keep everyone happy! Amazing with cheese, meat or just on the end of your finger.

```
Makes 4 jam-sized jars

800g ripe tomatoes (we use large vine
   tomatoes)
4 red chillis, with seeds
3 thumb-sized pieces of fresh ginger,
   peeled and chopped
8 garlic cloves, peeled
4 tablespoons fish sauce
450g caster sugar
150ml red wine vinegar
```

Put half the tomatoes, the chillies, ginger, garlic and fish sauce in a food processor and purée. Put the purée in a large pan with the sugar and vinegar and bring slowly to the boil, stirring, then reduce to a simmer.

Cut the remaining tomatoes into small dice and add them to the pan. Skim off the foam and simmer gently for 1½ hours, stirring and scraping the bottom of the pan every now and then.

Pour the jam into sterilised glass jars and let it cool at room temperature. The jam will keep in the fridge for weeks.

Who's afraid of a fiery soup?
— Pumpkin and Ginger

This soup was one of the first things we stirred and blended when we started hosting our supper club nights a few years ago, and it remains a startlingly popular choice whoever our guests are. Down on the market, we bought pumpkins by the bagful, chucked them and handfuls of fresh ginger into bags then ran back upstairs where we referred to a few cupboard staples to help the two come together. It's the secret ingredients – tabasco, fish and soy sauce – that really make the relationship work. Just make sure not to overdo it – you shouldn't be able to discern the last two in particular.

Serves 6—8

```
Glug of groundnut or sunflower oil
1 large onion, peeled and finely chopped
2 garlic cloves, crushed
2 thumbs-sized pieces of fresh ginger, peeled
    and finely chopped, plus extra for serving
750g pumpkin, peeled, deseeded and diced
1 large sweet potato, peeled and diced
50g creamed coconut, grated
1 teaspoon ground allspice
1 litre vegetable stock
Long dash of soy sauce
Long glug of fish sauce
Long glug of Tabasco
400g tin coconut milk
Salt and pepper
```

Heat the oil in a large pan or flameproof casserole on a low heat and fry the onion, garlic and ginger until soft. Add the pumpkin and sweet potato to sweat, followed by the creamed coconut and allspice. Stir well and add the stock. Bring to the boil, then cover and simmer for 15 minutes, stirring occasionally. Turn off the heat and add the soy sauce, fish sauce and Tabasco. Leave to cool a little, then add the coconut milk. Liquidise in a blender or food processor until smooth, season to taste and serve in deep bowls with crusty bread and a generous sprinkling of finely chopped ginger.

A thick, quick soup supper
— *Tomato, Herb and Sourdough*

A frying pan of tomatoes lies splattering on the hob while the evening news rolls on in the background and damp shoes and socks are taken off to be replaced by slippers. A meal alone or with friends lies ahead on a weekday evening and calls for something simple but filling that won't break the bank. This recipe makes lunch for four, or a hearty supper for one and a couple of desk lunches. Alternatively, freeze the left-overs and enjoy at a late date.

Serves 4

Glug of olive oil
½ white onion, finely sliced
2 garlic cloves, crushed
6-7 medium tomatoes, quartered
400g tin plum tomatoes
1 tablespoon sugar
Good glug of balsamic vinegar
250ml vegetable stock
2 thick slices of stale sourdough bread, cubed
Handful of fresh parsley, roughly chopped
Handful of fresh basil, torn
Salt and pepper
Grated hard cheese, to serve

Heat a glug of olive oil in a non-stick frying pan and sweat the onions for 5–10 minutes. Add the garlic, season generously and stir for a couple of minutes. Add both types of tomato, squeezing the tinned ones through your hand and into the pan. Follow with the sugar, balsamic vinegar and stock. Bring to a bubbling boil, then reduce to a simmer.

Crush the tomatoes with the back of a wooden spoon and allow to thicken for 10–15 minutes. Throw in half of the bread and continue to reduce, stirring occasionally. Tear in over half of the herbs then blitz very briefly in a liquidiser or with a hand-held blender to a coarse soup. Serve with the rest of the herbs, the remaining cubes of bread and a grated hard cheese if you have any.

Soup to the power of chowder
— *Smoked Haddock, King Prawn and Sweet Potato*

Rosie's husband must take the credit for this amazing chowder recipe. We first stole it for a residency at a local café where it featured on the lunch menu – proving so popular we ran out halfway through service and had the local fish monger running around the market in search of more smoked haddock for the pot. Chowder is traditionally a very thick and hearty soup so you don't need a huge bowl to fill you up and stay warm.

We sometimes add the flesh of 2 charred red peppers and omit the prawns for a more frugal version but here's the original in all its glory.

Serves 6

Glug of olive oil
2 white onions, peeled and sliced
1 large red chilli, deseeded and sliced (keep
  some seeds if you like the heat)
2 garlic cloves, peeled and sliced
1 large glass white wine
250ml fish stock
400g tin chopped tomatoes
2 large sweet potatoes, peeled and chopped
2 smoked haddock fillets, skinned and chopped
  into large chunks
1 teaspoon cayenne pepper
1 teaspoon paprika
½ teaspoon smoked paprika
12 raw peeled king prawns
2 tablespoons crème fraîche
Handful of chopped parsley
Salt and pepper

Warm a glug of olive oil in a deep pan and add the onion. Once soft and starting to colour, add the chilli and garlic and cook for a further minute. Add the wine, stock, tomatoes, sweet potatoes and half of the smoked haddock. Simmer for 25 minutes until the sweet potato is soft.

Add the cayenne pepper, paprika and smoked paprika and season to taste. Blitz with a hand blender until smooth (be careful of hot chowder flying up onto your arms and scalding while you whiz – this has been known to happen so take precautions!).

Add the remaining haddock then 2 minutes later add the king prawns and simmer for 3–4 minutes until the fish is cooked. Remove from heat, stir in the crème fraîche and serve with a sprinkling of chopped parsley.

Hot wasabi nights
— *Wasabi Beef Ramen*

You probably wouldn't be attempting this recipe unless you liked a shocking wasabi rush up the nose. We can't get enough and it needn't be reserved for sushi. Beef and horseradish are made for each other and marinating beef with wasabi (Japanese horseradish) and stirring some into this ramen broth make for an addictive and warming supper.

```
Enough for 4 deep bowls

500g rump steak
1 large thumb-sized piece of fresh ginger,
  grated*
3 tablespoons grated wasabi or wasabi paste
4 garlic cloves, crushed
1 tablespoon sesame oil
1 large red chilli, chopped
1.5 litres beef or chicken stock
5 tablespoons soy sauce
3 tablespoons fish sauce
200g flat rice or egg noodles
3 heads of pak choi, leaves separated
  and washed

To serve
2 spring onions, sliced diagonally
Handful of chopped coriander
Sesame seeds
Wasabi
Soy sauce
```

Rub the steaks all over with half each of the ginger, wasabi, garlic and sesame oil. Cover and leave in the fridge for 1–2 hours, or overnight. Remove the steaks from the fridge at least 30 minutes before cooking.

Heat the remaining sesame oil in a deep pan and add the remaining ginger, wasabi and garlic along with the chilli. When everything is sizzling, add the stock, soy and fish sauce and bring to a simmer.

Cook the noodles according to the packed instructions, refresh and set aside.

Heat a griddle pan over a medium-high heat. When the pan is hot, add the steaks and push down. Cook for 2 minutes, turn, season and cook for a further 2 minutes. Turn, season again and remove to a board to rest covered with foil and a tea towel.

Add the noodles and pak choi to the pan of broth and simmer for 4 minutes. Ladle the ramen into bowls, top with

slices of the beef, spring onions, coriander and sesame seeds. Allow people to season with wasabi and soy at the table.

*Ellie's Hot Tip – keep thumbs of ginger in the freezer until you need them; they can then be grated really easily straight into dishes like this.

A stylish veggie thali
— *Sweet Pumpkin Curry, Coconut Okra and Quick Chapati*

These recipes belong to a young woman in Madurai, Rajasthan, where Ellie spent an afternoon sitting on the kitchen floor of a family-run restaurant learning how to cook by pressure cooker.

Serves 4

For the pumpkin
Peanut or groundnut oil, for frying
1 teaspoon cumin seeds
1 teaspoon mustard seeds
450g pumpkin, peeled and cubed
½ white onion, peeled and finely chopped
1 garlic clove, finely chopped
1 thumb-sized piece of fresh ginger,
   peeled and finely chopped
½ teaspoon chilli powder
½ teaspoon salt
1 teaspoon garam masala
½ teaspoon turmeric
½ teaspoon coriander seeds
½ teaspoon aniseed
1 teaspoon sugar
½ 400g tin coconut milk
Handful fresh mint, roughly chopped
Natural or Greek-style yogurt, to serve

For the okra
250g okra, topped and tailed and cut into
   roughly 2cm lengths
Peanut or groundnut oil, for frying
1 teaspoon cumin seeds
1 teaspoon mustard seeds
450g pumpkin, peeled and cubed
½ white onion, peeled and finely chopped
1 garlic clove, finely cut
1 thumb-sized piece of fresh ginger, peeled
   and finely chopped
½ teaspoon chilli powder
½ teaspoon salt
1 teaspoon garam masala
½ teaspoon turmeric
½ teaspoon coriander seeds
Handful of dessicated coconut

For the chapati
1 glass plain flour
Couple of splashes of water
3 pinches salt

For the pumpkin, heat the oil in a deep pan and add the cumin and mustard seeds. Stir as they release their scent, then add the pumpkin, onion, garlic and ginger. Sweat on a low heat until softened, then add the chilli powder, salt, garam masala, turmeric, coriander, aniseed and sugar. Srir and add the coconut milk. Turn the heat to high so that it bubbles, then back to low and mash the with a fork.

For the okra, follow the same method as the pumpkin (omitting the aniseed, sugar or coconut milk). Before serving, scatter over the dessicated coconut.

For the chapatis, bring together the ingredients in a bowl or on a clean work surface using your hand in a claw shape, adding drops of water as necessary. Roll into golf ball-sized pieces, then flatten with a rolling pin. Dust each side with flour, then place onto a hot, dry griddle for a minute on each side, then lift with tongs into the flame until it flares up briefly and is nicely charred. Scatter the pumpkin and okra with fresh mint and serve with yogurt.

Time for a smoke
— *Jerk Salmon*

This recipe was one of the very first to grace our blog and Rosie's eye-popping marinade has since been slathered over shoulders of pork, slow-roasted at our supper club, and spread over countless chicken legs blackened on summer barbecues. Feel free to use this recipe to jerk whatever the hell you like but if you fancy a fishy supper with bite, a crisped fillet of jerk salmon, charred at the edges and meltingly tender within, is pretty hard to beat. Serve with a side of spinach and grated carrot salad or Seeded Cabbage Slaw (see page 142).

```
Serves 4

4 large salmon fillets

For the marinade
1 tablespoon ground allspice
½ tablespoon ground nutmeg
½ tablespoon black peppercorns
½ tablespoon dark brown sugar
4 cloves
Large pinch sea salt
4 garlic cloves, peeled and finely chopped
6 spring onions, roughly sliced
1 Scotch Bonnet chilli, with seeds (deseed
  if you can't handle the heat)
Large handful of fresh thyme leaves
1 tablespoon dark rum
1 tablespoon malt vinegar
Juice of 1 lime and a little zest
Groundnut oil
```

Blitz all the marinade ingredients except the groundnut oil in a food processor and then gradually add the groundnut oil until you have a coarse paste. Spread over the salmon fillets and leave to marinate for as long as you can.

Preheat a frying pan over a medium-high heat and add a drizzle of groundnut oil. Once the oil is hot, slide in the salmon fillets, skin side down, and fry for 6–8 minutes until the skin is crisped. Gently flip the fillets and fry for a further 5 minutes until cooked through and no longer translucent. Serve with plenty of cold Red Stripe.

Put a lid on it
— One Pot Chicken with Tarragon and Fresh Watercress Salad

The day we got going on painting our new shop we couldn't stop thinking about roast chicken. The weather was lurching between fits of sunshine and purple rain clouds and seemed to be asking for something light and warm on the table. With little time to cook for friends once the paintbrushes had been cleaned, Ellie thought back to a pot of roasted chicken a friend of her mum's had brought round, where all the ingredients were tucked in under the bird, and the whole thing was carved from the pot. With everything safely under a lid in the oven, we'd made time to dash into the shower and out of our painting clothes before supper was ready.

Serves 4

For the chicken
Glug of olive oil
1 medium white onion, finely chopped
1 celery stick, finely chopped
1 small carrot, peeled and finely chopped
2 or 3 bay leaves
6 rashers smoky streaky bacon, cut into
   thin pieces
1 free range whole chicken
1 large glass of white wine
1.5 litres vegetable stock
2 handfuls closed cup mushrooms, scrubbed
   and quartered
Handful of new or baby potatoes, scrubbed
   and halved (or quartered if they're large)
Handful of fresh tarragon
Salt and pepper

For the salad
Glug of white wine or cider vinegar
1 teaspoon Dijon mustard
Drizzle of olive oil
Big pinch of salt
Bag of watercress

Preheat the oven to 200°C/gas mark 6. Heat the olive oil in a flameproof casserole large enough to hold the chicken, and sweat the sofrito (onion, celery, carrot and bay). Once soft, add the bacon and stir to separate the pieces and stop them from catching. Cook for a few minutes, then introduce the chicken to the pot, topside down. Press down to seal the skin and keep in place. After a few minutes, turn the chicken bottom side down and repeat.

Add a glass of white wine to the pot along with the stock, mushrooms and potatoes. Pinch a few tarragon leaves from their stem and add, with a few twists from the salt and pepper mills. Bring the pot to the boil, then reduce to a simmer. Put a lid on the pot and place on the centre shelf of the oven. Cook for an hour, turning the chicken carefully after 30 minutes and making sure to baste it frequently. After an hour, remove the lid and let the stock reduce down. The chicken is ready when a skewer to the leg joint runs with clear juices. Lift the bird from the pot and place in a broad, rimmed serving bowl. Spoon over the vegetables and plenty of gravy, and finish with a scattering of torn tarragon.*

To make the salad, whisk together the vinegar, mustard, olive oil and salt and pour over the watercress just before eating – the balance should be acidic. Soak up the salad and chicken juices with thick bread.

*There will be a lot of stock left in the pan. Keep it back, along with any leftover chicken meat and vegetables and boil it up the next day with handful of risotto rice. Either eat as a soup or allow the stock to reduce right down into a risotto. Serve with grated Parmesan and a final finish of tarragon.

Put a lid on it again
— Lamb, Squash and Orzo Stew with Minted Yogurt

The second of this season's one pot wonders was a delicious Greek-inspired lamb, squash and orzo stew. Tender, rich and sweet and very hard to stop scooping up by the spoonful. You may sniff at using dried mint in the minted yogurt but it works far better than fresh in delivering a cooling punch to counterbalance the richness of the stew.

Serves 4

Glug of olive oil
2 onions, peeled and sliced
2 cinnamon sticks
Pinch dried oregano (or fresh if you can find)
Leaves from 2 thyme sprigs
1kg lamb shoulder, cut into roughly 4cm cubes
  and trimmed of excess fat
400g tin plum or cherry tomatoes
Lamb stock (see right)
400g squash, peeled and cut into large cubes
200g orzo
Handful of grated Parmesan
Salt and pepper

Minted yogurt
Greek or natural yogurt
1 tablespoon dried mint
1 teaspoon white wine vinegar

Preheat the oven to 160°C/gas mark 3. Warm a glug of olive oil in a large flameproof casserole and add the onions, cinnamon sticks, oregano and thyme. Once the onions start to soften, add the lamb and stir. Once lightly browned, add a big pinch of salt and some pepper.

Add the tomatoes and top the pan up with stock* until the meat is just submerged. Cover the pan and place in the oven for 2 hours.

Forty minutes before the end of cooking time, stir in the squash, re-cover and return to the oven. Twenty minutes before the end of cooking time, do the same with the orzo. Once 2 hours is up, remove from the oven, grate over some Parmesan and leave to cool for 5–10 minutes.

Mix the yogurt, mint and vinegar in a bowl and serve with the pot of stew.

Quick Lamb Stock

If you're asking your butcher to dice and trim the lamb shoulder for you, ask if you can keep the bones for the stock pot. The same goes for any bones really, and that include stripped roast chicken carcass from Sunday's lunch.

Put the bones in a saucepan with 1 litre of cold water, around 10 peppercorns and 2 large pinches of salt and bring slowly to the boil. Then add any of the following that need using up from your vegetable drawer or herb garden.

Leek ends
Thyme sprigs
Bay leaves
Carrots
Courgettes
Onions
Celery
Parsley stalks

Simmer for 2 hours, skimming off any froth every now and then. Strain through a sieve and use as needed.

A frugal lunch with friends
— *Aubergine Stuffed with Ground Lamb*

Middle Eastern cooking is high on our list of influences, not least because the flavours are so punchy and the ingredients so easy to play with. We enjoy the respect for informal home cooking and the lack of fuss at the table – often it's just a case of roasting or grilling, then turning something out of its skin and binding loosely with a little yogurt, cheese or herbs. Eat this aubergine on its own or as part of a mezze meal.

Serves 2

1 large aubergine
Olive oil, for brushing and frying
½ medium white onion, finely chopped
100g lamb mince
1 heaped teaspoon cumin seeds
½ teaspoon ground cinnamon
½ teaspoon hot chilli powder
Halloumi (optional)
Pinch of sumac
Fresh herbs for scattering (e.g. mint,
   coriander and parsley), roughly chopped
Greek yogurt, to serve
Salt and pepper

Preheat the oven to 240°C/gas mark 9. Halve the aubergine lengthways and score the flesh in a criss cross pattern, taking care not to pierce through the skin. Brush with a little oil and season generously. Bake on a high shelf for 30–40 minutes until the flesh has collapsed and the skin has crisped.

Heat a little olive oil in a frying pan and soften the onions. After a couple of minutes, add the lamb and spices and fry together over a low heat, breaking up the mince with a fork.

Scoop the aubergine flesh into a bowl, mashing it as you go, and combine with the lamb. Spoon back into the aubergine skins. At this point you could add a few thin slices of halloumi before placing under the grill for a few minutes, but it's just as good without.

Remove from the grill and scatter a little lemony sumac on top, along with the chopped herbs. Serve with a generous amount of Greek yogurt on the side.

Restorative supper for two tired parents
— *Sausages with Puy Lentils, Potatoes and Crème Fraîche*

The problem with sausage and mash is there's always too much mash and the problem with sausage and lentils is that there are usually too many lentils! This simple braise mixes both textures for a delicious and varied accompaniment to your bangers that keeps the taste buds stimulated until the very last forkful.

Serves 2

4 high pork content sausages
Splash of olive oil
Handful of thyme sprigs
150g Puy lentils
4 shallots
4 waxy potatoes
1 large red chilli, deseeded and sliced
3 garlic cloves, chopped
1 tablespoon fennel seeds
1 bay leaf
1 tablespoon red wine vinegar
500ml stock
2 tablespoons crème fraîche

Preheat the oven to 200°C/gas mark 6. Put the sausages in a baking tray with a splash of olive oil and some whole thyme sprigs and bake for 30–40 minutes, turning once, until browned all over.

Meanwhile, put the lentils in a pan, cover with cold water and bring to the boil. Drain and set aside.

Peel the shallots and separate into their smaller bulbs (or cut them in half if using larger shallots). Slice the potatoes into roughly 5mm slices.

Heat a little oil in an ovenproof frying pan over a medium heat and add the shallots, chilli and garlic. Cook for 5 minutes. Add the fennel seeds, bay leaf and potatoes and fry for another 5 minutes. Add the lentils and stock and simmer, partially covered, for about 30 minutes until the potatoes and lentils are tender. Turn off the heat and stir in the vinegar.

Put one tablespoon of crème fraîche in the centre of each bowl, ladle over the lentils and potatoes, stir lightly to combine and top with the sausages.

Sweet and sour supper hot from the Middle East
— *Lamb Kabob Cooked with Cherries*

This dish is the most celebrated – and recreated – of Syria's second biggest city, Aleppo, where it's eaten on piles of pitta cut into triangles and finished with toasted pine nuts and parsley. Nothing beats the sharp-sweet bite of the dark purple cherries and pomegranate molasses getting up close to the lamb meatballs. We're sure you'll find yourself hankering after it again before long.

Serves 4

400g lamb mince
1 small white onion, very finely chopped
  or coarsely grated
400g cherries
½ cup water
2 tablespoons pomegranate molasses
1 teaspoon cinnamon
½ teaspoon allspice
1 heaped teaspoon sugar
1 lemon
Olive oil, for frying
Handful of pine nuts
Knob of butter
Pitta bread, for serving
Handful of fresh parsley, chopped
Salt and pepper

Using your hands, mix the minced lamb with the onion and a generous dose of salt and pepper. Refrigerate for an hour if you have time – this will help firm up the meatballs.

Stone the cherries, being careful to catch the juices, and add to a large pan. Add the water, molasses, cinnamon, allspice, sugar and a squeeze of lemon. Bring to the boil, then simmer over a low-medium heat for 15 minutes until thickened. Stir the sauce and squash the fruit with a spoon.

Roll the mince meat into small balls a little larger than a marble using the flat of your palms. Warm a little oil in a frying pan and brown them on all sides. Add them with their juices to the cherry sauce and continue to simmer until the meat is cooked through.

Fry the pine nuts in butter until golden. Toast or grill a few pieces of pitta bread, then cut into triangular pieces. Arrange them on a plate with the pointed edges outwards and the rough sides upwards, then spoon the meatballs and their sauce over the top. Scatter with the buttery pine nuts and finish with parsley. Serve immediately.

Red hot smoky
— *Smoked Paprika Pork Chops with Celeriac and Butternut Rösti*

This bold pork marinade is not only great for adding flavour, it also turns the chops a wonderful bright paprika-stained red – you can tell how smoky and hot they're going to be just by looking at them. We use two of our favourite autumn roots in the rösti – earthy celeriac and sweet butternut – for a delicious and colourful alternative to potatoes.

Serves 2

2 pork chops on the bone, rind removed
    and excess fat trimmed

For the marinade
2 tablespoons smoked paprika
1 teaspoon mustard powder
1 tablespoon zatar (or dried thyme and
    crushed coriander seeds)
1 tablespoon soy sauce
Splash of groundnut oil
Salt and pepper

For the rösti
½ small celeriac
½ small butternut squash
Large knob of butter
Splash of olive oil
1 onion, finely sliced
Salt

Smother the chops with all the marinade ingredients after you have combined them together in a small bowl. Set aside for as long as you can (it's such a punchy marinade that 20–30 minutes should do it).

Meanwhile, peel and grate the celeriac and squash into a clean tea towel. Form into a sausage shape, scatter over some salt and roll up the tea towel as tight as you can over the sink, squeezing out any excess water.

Melt the butter with a splash of olive oil in a frying pan and, when gently bubbling, tip in the vegetables and onions. Stir to coat, flatten with the back of a spatula and leave to brown on the underside over a low heat for 10–15 minutes.

We managed to toss the rösti like a pancake but if you don't feel like taking a risk with your supper, flip it over with a spatula to brown on the other side. Once cooked through and browned, keep warm in the oven.

Open a window, brush a griddle pan lightly with groundnut oil and get it hot and smoky over a high heat. Slide in the pork chops and push down firmly with tongs. Turn down to medium and cook for 5–6 minutes each side, or until the juices run clear when you cut the fattest part of the chop near the bone. Serve with watercress and cold white wine.

Salad Club loves ragu
— *Pappardelle with Duck Ragu*

We love a ragu here at Salad Club. We've served up many different versions in the past – oxtail, venison, rabbit, beef and pork are all fine contenders but if the night feels particularly dark and you're hankering after one rich, silky mother of a ragu it has to be duck. Roasting the bird first renders the fat so you're left with tender strips of dark meat just crying out to be ragued.

Serves 4

1 free range duck crown (approx 1kg)
Handful of thyme sprigs
1 white onion
2 celery sticks
1 carrot
½ celeriac, peeled
Glug of olive oil
6 garlic cloves, peeled and finely sliced
2 tablespoons balsamic vinegar
Small glass of red wine
400ml chicken stock
400g tin plum tomatoes
500g dry pappardelle
Salt and pepper

To serve
Zest of 1 lemon
Parmesan

Preheat the oven to 180°C/gas mark 4. Spatchcock the duck, season all over and place on a baking tray on a bed of thyme sprigs, cover with foil and roast for 35–45 minutes.

Meanwhile finely dice or briefly blitz the onion, celery, carrot and celeriac in a food processor. Heat a long glug of olive oil in a wide pan over a medium heat, add the vegetables and a large pinch of salt and pepper. Cook gently for 10–15 minutes until soft and starting to colour. Turn up the heat and add the garlic, stir and cook for a further 2 minutes. Add the balsamic vinegar and red wine and stir for 2 minutes. Add the stock and tomatoes and reduce to a low simmer.

Remove the duck from the oven and let it rest for 5–10 minutes under foil. Remove the skin and shred the flesh. Add the duck to the pan along with the juices and a few of the thyme sprigs from the baking tray. Cover and leave to simmer gently while you cook the pasta.

Bring a large pan of water to a rolling boil, add salt and cook the pasta until al dente.

Once cooked, transfer the pasta to the ragu pan with a slotted spoon, bringing some of the pasta water with you as go to help loosen the sauce. Grate the lemon zest over the ragu and take to the table in the pan to serve up. Grate over plenty of Parmesan and complement with a hefty Italian red wine.

A hearty yet refreshing meal for chilly cooks
— *Warm Barley and Almond Tabbouleh with Pomegranate*
— *Pear and Goats' Cheese Tarts*

Warm Barley and Almond Tabbouleh with Pomegranate

We use barley rather than bulgar wheat in this warm, nutty autumn take on tabbouleh, but feel free to stick to cracked wheat if that's what you have in the cupboard. The warmth of the just-cooked grains infused with heady cinnamon and the sweet, toasty crunch of the almonds provide a steady surface warmth and depth for the fresh and vibrant flavours of pomegranate, lemon and yogurt to play around.

Serves 4

```
200g pearl barley
1 cinnamon stick
Juice and zest of 1 lemon
1 small red onion, finely sliced
1 large red chilli, finely sliced with
   a few seeds
Handful of fresh parsley, leaves and tender
   parts of stalks finley chopped
Handful of fresh coriander, leaves and tender
   parts of stalks finely chopped
1 celery stick, finely diced
5 tablespoons olive oil
Large handful of blanched or flaked almonds
   (blanched have more flavour)
Handful of shelled pistachios (optional)
Handful of pomegranate seeds
```

Put the barley and cinnamon stick in a saucepan, cover with water and bring to the boil. Simmer for 30 minutes until the barley is tender.

Meanwhile, juice the lemon into a bowl and add the onion, chilli, chopped herb stalks, celery and olive oil.

Toast the almonds in a dry pan over a medium heat until just starting to brown, then bash or chop them into small pieces with the pistachios, if you're using them.

Drain the barley and add it straight to the bowl while it's steaming, stir in the nuts and the herb leaves, scatter with pomegranate seeds and lemon zest and serve immediately.

Pear and Goats' Cheese Tarts

The recipe below makes 2 small tarts, each 10cm across. Just up the quantities if you want to make a few larger ones, or add wafer-thin slices of boiled beetroot for a flash of colour.

Serves 2

```
100g puff pastry, rolled out thinly and
   dusted with flour
1 pear
75g goats' cheese
Sprig of fresh thyme
Drizzle of honey
Salt and pepper
```

Preheat the oven to 180°C/gas mark 4. Use an upturned tart tin to cut out circles of pastry. Lay the pastry into each tin and press down. Halve, top and tail the pear, taking out the core as you go. Slice thinly and arrange with alternate slices of cheese in the pastry cases. Season and sprinkle with thyme leaves. Cook for 20 minutes until golden brown. Drizzle with honey and turn onto a plate. Eat with grapes and a green salad.

The perfect match
— *Chocolate, Orange and Beetroot Brownies*

The concept of using the natural juices of root veg to keep a cake moist and sweet is nothing groundbreaking, so we won't bang on about how clever it is. We will just say that these brownies have been met with rapture by even the staunchest of beetroot deriders. Orange is a good friend of both beetroot and chocolate and all of the flavours combine to make one hell of a good brownie.

Makes 1 large tray

3 small uncooked beetroots
250g good-quality dark chocolate (minimum
  70% cocoa solids)
250g unsalted butter
250g caster sugar
3 free range eggs
Zest of 1 orange and juice of half
160g self-raising flour
Crème fraîche, to serve

Boil up your beets for about 30 minutes until tender to the point of a knife, then peel, blitz to a purée in a food processor or blender and set aside.

Preheat the oven to 180°C/gas mark 4. Lightly butter and line a large baking tin at least 2cm deep.

Break the chocolate into pieces and place in a heatproof bowl over a pan of barely simmering water. Add the butter in cubes and leave to melt, stirring once or twice.

In another bowl, whisk the sugar with the eggs until smooth and creamy. Stir in the melted chocolate, orange zest and juice and puréed beetroot then sift in the flour and stir until combined.

Pour the mixture into the tin and bake for 15–20 minutes. If you plan to reheat the brownies before serving, stick to 15 minutes or even less if you like a gooey brownie! Serve with crème fraîche.

Kettle on, cakes in the oven
– Lemon, Yogurt and Blackberry Muffins

Rosie's allotment is heaving with ripe blackberries at the moment. You just have to rustle a branch for overflowing handfuls of them. These muffins are a perfect way to use them up and with the addition of yogurt and lemon, they're wonderfully light and zingy.

Makes 12 muffins

120g butter
120g caster sugar
1 free range egg
Zest of 1 lemon and juice of half
2 tablespoons Greek or natural yogurt
120g self raising flour
½ teaspoon baking powder
80g ground almonds
2 handfuls blackberries

Preheat the oven to at 180°C/gas mark 4. Beat the butter and sugar together until smooth then whisk in the egg, the lemon juice and zest and the yogurt.

Sift in the flour and baking powder and stir in the almonds until everything is well combined. Keep a few blackberries back to decorate the tops and stir in the rest, lightly crushing some between your fingers to release the juice.

Stir once and tip into paper cases placed in the holes of a muffin tray until roughly three-quarters full. Bake for 20–25 minutes until risen and golden.

Spice is nice
— *Banana Bread*

The first thing to say about banana bread is that it just doesn't work unless the bananas are completely ripe. An unripe banana doesn't yield properly to the pressure of a fork and certainly doesn't have much flavour. The pungent, almost petrol-like, pear-droppy flavour of a black-skinned banana is all we can ask for here. Buy them at the local shop and they'll be sure to be selling them off cheap. The condensed milk is a bit of a magic trick – it ensures the bread extra extra moist and chewy.

```
Makes 1 loaf

250g plain flour
1 teaspoon bicarbonate of soda
½ teaspoon salt
2 teaspoons ground nutmeg
1½ teaspoons ground ginger
Seeds of 5 cardamom pods
1½ teaspoons cinnamon
150g granulated sugar
100g unsalted butter, plus extra for buttering
2 free range eggs, lightly beaten
5 medium-sized very ripe bananas, mashed
397g tin condensed milk
1 teaspoon vanilla extract
```

Preheat the oven to 180°C/gas mark 4. Add all the dry ingredients except the sugar to a bowl and loosely bring together. In a separate bowl, beat together the sugar and butter, then add the eggs. Continue whisking and add the banana, condensed milk and vanilla extract. Stir well, then gently fold in the dry ingredients with a wooden spoon. Butter and line a loaf tin and pour in the mixture. Cook for 55 minutes until golden brown, testing the centre with a wooden skewer (it should come out clean.) If the edges of the cake are nearing too brown, remove from the oven and allow to cool. The cake will set as it does so.

Teatime and the leaves are falling
— *Apricot, Pistachio and Almond Flapjacks*

Flapjacks are an autumn staple – it's always good to reach into the biscuit tin on the way out of the door and grab something sustaining and satisfyingly chewy.

Makes 24 flapjacks

400g whole rolled oats
150g dried apricots, roughly chopped
40g mixed seed (we use sesame, pumpkin
 and sunflower)
40g whole almonds, roughly chopped
40g whole pistachios, roughly chopped
100g butter
2 heaped tablespoons tahini
3 heaped tablespoons golden syrup
50g granulated sugar

Preheat the oven to 160°C/gas mark 3. Combine the dry ingredients except the sugar in a mixing bowl and set aside. Add the butter, tahini, syrup and sugar to a pan on a low heat. Stir to melt the butter and sugar, then add to the mixing bowl. Turn well to mix the two. Grease an ovenproof dish or baking tray and turn the mixture into it, pressing down firmly. Bake for 25 minutes until dark golden brown. Remove and slice straight away – the flapjacks will firm up as they cool.

What's in a crumble?
— *Plum and Ginger*

We've learned over the years that crumbles mean different things to different people. To some they are an unwelcome reminder of school meals and tepid yellow custard covered in a thick film – a dessert to be avoided at all costs. To others they are the shimmering beacon of all puddings – a British classic that really comes into its own when autumn bears its fruits: apple and blackberry, pear and rhubarb, and this vibrant plum and ginger number.

Serves 4–6

12 plums
1 tablespoon vanilla sugar
2 tablespoons golden caster sugar
  (plus extra for plums if needed)
6 ginger biscuits
Small handful of crystallised ginger
1 tablespoon ground ginger
100g flour
50g butter
2 tablespoons ground almonds
Single cream, to serve

Preheat the oven to 180°C/gas mark 4. Stone and halve the plums and toss with the vanilla sugar in a small baking dish. Leave to infuse.

Blitz the remaining ingredients in a food processor until they're the texture of coarse breadcrumbs.

Test the plums for sweetness and add a little golden caster sugar to taste. Top the plums with the crumble mixture, sprinkle with a little more sugar and bake for 30–40 minutes until golden and crisp on top. Serve with lashings of single cream.

Autumn's birthday cake
— *Flourless Chocolate, Prune and Brandy Cake*

There's no flour to help this cake rise, which means it has all the space in the world to get on and show off its chocolatey credentials. Wet and ganachey, it's impossible not to sink your teeth into a sliver of the good stuff and savour the way it sticks to the roof of your mouth. This is the king of chocolate cakes and should be made for special people only! We hope that this page in your book will become quite chocolate-covered in time.

Serves 10

```
100g prunes, roughly chopped
100ml brandy
250g good-quality dark chocolate (minimum
    70% cocoa solids)
225g butter
200g light muscovado sugar
4 free range eggs, separated
Crème fraîche or mascarpone, to serve
```

Preheat the oven to 160°C/gas mark 3. Butter a non-stick cake tin and line with a circle of greaseproof paper. We use a 22cm loose-bottomed one but a similar size is fine. Soak the prunes in brandy in a small bowl and melt the chocolate and butter in a heatproof bowl over a saucepan of barely simmering water.

In a large mixing bowl, whisk the sugar and egg yolks together. Fold in the melted chocolate.

Whisk the egg whites in a separate bowl until white and frothy – this should take at least 5 minutes. Add the brandy-soaked prunes to the chocolate mix, and then gently fold in the egg whites.

Tip into the cake tin and bake slowly for 40–45 minutes. Use a skewer to test the centre of the cake, then allow to cool before carefully slipping onto a plate. Serve in thin slivers with crème fraîche or mascarpone.

Winter

Winter

Now that we've come to the end of writing this chapter and spring is in the air, winter's stomach-warming recipes are all looking mighty fine. The reality is that it's been hard and we've had to find ways to cheer up our kitchens while we write. However, as the kitchen warms up, so do we; there's actually no better place when it's cold outside than near a warm oven or a bubbling pot. While the list of ingredients from duck and black pudding to thyme and fennel is inviting, rich and comforting, there's no way we could eat these all year round and stay happy. The real pleasure of hearty, fiery, soulful dishes is knowing that they're for a limited time only, and like bargain basement shops at sale time, EVERYTHING MUST GO!

Winter is the season for huddling together at the kitchen table, drinking lots of wine, tearing loaves of bread and scooping up countless hot mouthfuls of something informally plonked in the middle – be it stew, curry, gratin, a trio of winter salads, or fat, juicy slices of a roasted bird. Winter is about getting a bit primal, meaty and manly – all things we're quite fond of.

For us, the season's relentless gloom is made manageable by what we eat, and barely allowing ourselves to look up from our plates and the confines of our ovens to check the skies around us. Months of wool-lined boots, oversized hats and pots of gut-expanding stew can only be tolerated for a limited period. Unlike in the summer months, when meals can be thrown together quickly without too much thought, the process of winter cooking requires a little more attention to avoid eating the same old comforting staples night after night. The fact that we make time for braising, roasting and boiling proves just how much we need the soul-warming hunks of tender meat, red wine stews and softened root vegetables to keep us going.

A Menu for Winter

Breakfast & Brunch

...

Kedgeree with Poached Eggs and Watercress &
Crumbed Kedgeree and Fontina Rice Balls

Winter Salads & Lunches

...

Jerusalem Artichoke and Sesame Remoulade
Tenderstem Broccoli with Prunes and Bacon
Aromatic Roast Duck and Pancakes with 'Homestyle' Cabbage
Beetroot with Chorizo, Feta and Mint
Giant Couscous, Butternut and Walnut Salad with Pomegranate
Seeded Cabbage Slaw
Warm Mackerel and Beetroot Niçoise
Allspice Buttered Chicken with Pistachio, Sultana and
Rose Pilaf with Nigella Lebneh
Alternative birds
Green Lentils and Spelt with Fennel, Fresh Herbs and French
Vinaigrette
Warm Fennel with Goats' Cheese, Olives, Capers and Pine Nuts

Hearty Winter Suppers

...

Sweet Potato, Fennel and Smoked Bacon Gratin
Melanzane
Salted Pork Belly Stew with Black Pudding,
Chorizo and Butter Beans
Beef, Ginger and Coconut Curry with Coriander Rice
Ultimate Veggie Chilli

Toad-in-the-Hole with Pancetta and Red Onion Gravy
Italian Peasants' Soup or Ribollita
Gin and Juniper Pork with Leek and Parmesan Stuffed Squash

Something Sweet / To Drink

...

Chocolate and Hazelnut Swirls
Vanilla Pear Pancakes with Hazelnut Mascarpone
Chilli Chocolate Pots
Four Affogatos
Chocolate, Apricot and Ginger Cake

Winter weekend brunch
— *Kedgeree with Poached Eggs and Watercress*
— *Crumbled Kedgeree and Fontina Rice Balls*

When you feel like taking your time over a hearty brunch, there's nothing better or more restorative than a steaming bowl of kedgeree, a dish introduced to the breakfast table in Victorian times by colonials returning from India. The smell of curry powder wafting through the hallways late morning is evocative of many a school lunch.

Traditional kedgeree includes hard-boiled eggs, to which we're not averse as long as the yolks are soft and the whites are bright, but topping the curried rice and fish with peppery watercress and a perfectly poached egg is even better. Plus it skips out all that fiddly egg peeling. Having run out of basmati, Rosie used risotto rice in this recipe with great results. Feel free to use up any rice you may have knocking around in the cupboard.

Serves 4

Glug of olive oil
1 large white onion, finely sliced
2 tablespoons curry powder
300g risotto rice (we use Carnaroli)
6–8 coriander stalks, finely chopped
125ml white wine
800ml chicken or vegetable stock
Knob of butter
100g frozen peas
1 large, un-dyed smoked haddock fillet,
  skinned and diced
4 free range eggs

To serve
2 spring onions, finely sliced
Handful of coriander leaves, chopped
4 heaped tablespoons Greek yogurt
4 tablespoons Mango chutney (shop bought
  is fine)
4 handfuls of watercress
Pepper

Add a generous glug of olive oil to a large, high-sided frying pan over a medium heat, then add the onion and stir occasionally until soft and translucent (about 10 minutes). Add the curry powder, stir, then add the rice and coriander stalks and stir again until all the rice is coated. Pour in the wine and scrape the bottom of the pan to deglaze then stir until all the liquid is absorbed. Turn down the heat and add

a ladle of stock. You don't have to stir all the time if the heat is on low, just keep an eye on the pan and stir occasionally. Once the first lot of stock has been absorbed, add another ladle and repeat until the rice is tender, adding more water if necessary.

Once the rice is tender, add the butter, peas and fish, stir once, turn off the heat and leave, covered, for 10 minutes. This gives the kedgeree time to become amazingly creamy as the steam from the hot rice gently cooks the fish and peas.

Meanwhile, bring a pan of salted water to a rolling boil. Crack each egg into a tea cup and tip them into the boiling water one by one. Turn off the heat, cover and leave for 4 minutes. (There are many different ways to poach an egg but we find this has the most successful results. The most important thing is to buy really fresh eggs so that the whites stay solid around the yolk rather than turning into floaty ghosts!)

To serve, spoon the kedgeree into shallow bowls and sprinkle with the spring onions and coriander. Top with dollops of Greek yogurt and mango chutney, pile on a handful of watercress and finish with the poached egg and some black pepper.

Crumbled Kedgeree and Fontina Rice Balls
If you've got leftover kedgeree from our recipe above, these fried rice balls make impressive canapés or starters. In fact you can have them any time you like. This recipe works well with any leftover risotto or rice dish, either fried on its own or filled with your favourite soft cheese for a melting middle.

Leftover kedgeree, chilled
100g Fontina cheese
1 free range egg, beaten
Breadcrumbs (Japanese Panko are very good
  for this)
Groundnut oil, for frying

Be prepared to get your hands dirty! Fill you palm with a layer of kedgeree, pile a dollop of Fontina into the centre, cover with more kedgeree and mould into a ball. Gently roll the rice ball in the beaten egg, then in the breadcrumbs. Repeat until all the kedgeree or rice is used up.

Heat half a centimetre of groundnut oil in a non-stick frying pan and, when the oil is smoking and hot, add the rice balls and fry on all sides until golden brown. Drain on kitchen towel, allow to cool slightly, then serve.

Alternative winter salads and side plates
— *Jerusalem Artichoke and Sesame Remoulade*
— *Tenderstem Broccoli with Prunes and Bacon*

Jerusalem Artichoke and Sesame Remoulade

We were new to Jerusalem artichokes this winter, and look forward to listing their merits further next year. The first time we tried them it seemed obvious to match them with a dry, sesame dressing that would add to their distinct artichoke-y nuttiness.

Serve with bread and Serrano ham for a light Saturday lunch, or with Seeded Cabbage Slaw (see page 142).

Serves 6

2 tablespoons tahini paste
Glug of grassy olive oil
6 Jerusalem artichokes, peeled and cut
  into fine matchsticks
1 tablespoon sesame seeds
Salt and pepper

In a small bowl, whisk together the tahini and olive oil. Season and set aside. Bring a small saucepan of salted water to a rolling boil and add the artichoke matchsticks. Boil until just tender, then drain and refresh under a cold tap and turn with the dressing onto a plate. Warm the sesame seeds in a dry skillet and scatter over the remoulade. Serve immediately.

Tenderstem Broccoli with Prunes and Bacon

As this dish was born from one of our favourite 1980s canapés, Devils on Horseback, we thought we should call it Devils on Horseback in the Woods. Eat as part of a group of salads or on your own for a midweek supper. You could even top it off with a poached egg if you feel so inclined. Use regular broccoli if you can't find the sprouting or tenderstem variety, though this is far more elegant on the plate.

Serves 2

6 prunes, roughly chopped
100g pancetta or smoked bacon, diced
2 handfuls tenderstem broccoli
Small block of Parmesan, for shaving
Splash of white wine vinegar
Squeeze of lemon juice
1 teaspoon English mustard
Olive oil, to loosen

Heat the prunes and pancetta in a dry frying pan until warm, sticky and browned. Bring a pan of well-salted water up to a rolling boil and plunge the broccoli in for 3 minutes. Transfer to the frying pan for a minute or two, then to the plate with a few shavings of Parmesan. Combine the vinegar, lemon juice, mustard and oil in a cup and dress the salad. Serve immediately.

A long and late weekend lunch
— *Aromatic Roast Duck with Pancakes*
— *Homestyle Cabbage*

Aromatic Roast Duck with Pancakes

A recent trip to Chinatown in London inspired this home recipe for crispy aromatic duck. Don't be put off by the long ingredients list! This recipe is far less fiddly than the traditional method of steaming and deep-fat frying, and everything can be cooked in one tray. The cloves, cinnamon and orange give this dish a very festive feel so it's a great alternative to the celebration.

We're lucky enough to have an Asian supermarket nearby but if you can't get to one, large supermarkets now stock a broad range of Asian products so you should be able to find what you need. Otherwise there are some brilliant online suppliers such as www.waiyeehong.com.

The 'homestyle' cabbage served alongside the duck is a tribute to a dish of the same name from our local Xinjiang restaurant where everything is cooked and served with insane – and addictive – quantities of chilli and garlic.

Serves 4 as a main course, 6 as a starter

For the marinade
100ml chicken or vegetable stock
3 tablespoons Szechuan peppercorns
1 tablespoon coriander seeds
2 cinnamon sticks
5 star anise
6 spring onions
6 garlic cloves
8 tablespoons Chinese rice wine
  (sake or gin are ideal alternatives)
3cm piece of fresh root ginger, peeled
  and chopped

For the duck
2kg free range, oven-ready duck
  (giblets removed)
2 tablespoons sea salt
1 orange

To serve
18 Chinese-style pancakes
Hoisin sauce
6 spring onions, sliced
½ cucumber, cut into matchsticks

Blitz all the marinade ingredients in a food processor until you have a coarse paste, adding a splash more rice wine if it looks too dry.

Heat the oven to 120°C/gas mark ½. Wash the duck inside and out and dry thoroughly with kitchen towel. Put your fingers or a blunt knife under the skin and pull it away from the flesh to loosen it (this will help it crisp). Rub the sea salt all over the skin and inside the cavity. Cut the orange in half and cut the peel into strips, then put both halves and the peel inside the duck. Put some marinade under the skin where you loosened it then rub the rest all over the duck. Pour the stock into the cavity, cover with foil and roast for 2 hours.

Turn the oven to max, remove the foil and roast for another 40 minutes, then let it rest under foil for 20 minutes. Remove all the skin, slice the skin and return it to the oven to crisp further. Meanwhile, roughly carve and shred the duck onto a plate. Steam or microwave the pancakes and serve with the hoisin, the sliced spring onions and cucumber and let everyone assemble their own pancakes.

Homestyle Cabbage

2 tablespoons rice vinegar
2 tablespoons soy sauce
1 tablespoon caster sugar
2 tablespoons sesame oil
1 red chilli, sliced, with seeds
3 garlic cloves, peeled and sliced
1 green pointed cabbage, cut into large slices

Mix the rice vinegar, soy sauce and sugar together to make the dressing. Heat the sesame oil in a wok or large frying pan. Add the chilli, garlic and cabbage and stir fry over a high heat for about 5 minutes until the green of the cabbage has darkened but the leaves still retain their bite. Dress and serve immediately.

You can add thin strips of carrot or lightly steamed broccoli to this recipe and a sprinkling of roasted peanuts to make it more substantial.

Long ladies' lunch: a trio of winter salads
— *Beetroot with Chorizo, Feta and Mint*
— *Giant Couscous, Butternut and Walnut*
— *Seeded Cabbage Slaw*

Beetroot with Chorizo, Feta and Mint

We use chorizo everywhere because it has such a strong presence and is really versatile. In this salad it oozes its rust-coloured oils to combine with the earthy, salty and fresh flavours of its counterparts. Luxurious.

Serves 6

```
2 medium uncooked beetroot
2 regular sausage-sized chorizo picante
(uncured), sliced into rounds, then
quartered
1 tablespoon balsamic vinegar
Pinch of salt
100g feta cheese
Handful of mint, loosely chopped
Drizzle of olive oil
```

Remove the beetroot leaves, being careful not to cut too close to the bulb, and boil the beets for 45 minutes. Drain, peel and finely slice.

Add the chorizo to a hot frying pan and keep an eye on it while laying the beetroot slices out on a large plate or platter.

Lightly toss the beetroot with the balsamic and a pinch of salt. Once the chorizo has crisped, tip it over the beetroot with the oil. Crumble over the feta in large chunks and finish with the mint. Drizzle with olive oil and serve immediately.

Giant Couscous, Butternut and Walnut

Giant (or Israeli pearl) couscous is a very quick and useful cupboard staple to throw into soups or salads and has a springy texture totally unlike the sandy grains of standard couscous. If you can't find it, barley, spelt or orzo pasta are good substitutes.

Serves 6

```
1 large butternut squash, seeded and cut
  into small dice
Long glug of good olive oil
½ teaspoon chilli powder
400g giant couscous
Heaped handful of walnut pieces, broken
½ pomegranate, seeds and juices reserved
½ lemon
Handful of mint, roughly chopped
```

Preheat the oven to 200°C/gas mark 6 and tip the squash into a roasting tin. Drizzle with olive oil and add the chilli powder, using your hands to coat evenly. Roast until softened and crisp at the edges, and allow to cool.

Boil the couscous for 5–10 minutes in well-salted water, until al dente. Drain and refresh under a cold tap, drizzling with a little oil to prevent sticking. When the couscous and squash are both cooled, add to a serving bowl and stir once.

Add the walnut pieces and deep red pomegranate seeds and juices, then turn gently to combine. Just before serving, squeeze the lemon half through your hands over the salad, dress with olive oil and turn again with the mint. Scoop up with baby gem leaves, radicchio or hot pitta breads.

Seeded Cabbage Slaw

The yogurt adds a pleasing tang to the smoky nigella seeds hidden in the cabbage. This slaw is predictably good between bread with cold meat and mango chutney.

Serves 6

```
½ head red cabbage, sliced very thinly
½ head white cabbage, sliced very thinly
1 medium red onion, sliced very thinly
2 carrots, grated
Handful of sesame seeds, lightly toasted
Handful of black onion or nigella seeds
Handful of mint, chopped
Handful of coriander, chopped
```

```
For the dressing
2 tablespoons natural or Greek yogurt
Juice of ½ lemon
Heaped teaspoon of grain mustard
Heaped teaspoon of English mustard
Glug of red or white wine vinegar
Salt and pepper
```

To make the dressing, whisk together the yogurt, lemon juice, both mustards, vinegar and seasoning. Taste and adjust to suit. It should be pretty punchy.

Add the shredded vegetables to a large serving bowl. Pour over the dressing and turn well with a small handful of sesame seeds and black onion seeds. Finish with a scattering of mint and coriander and serve immediately.

A colourful lunch on a dreary day
— *Warm Mackerel and Beetroot Niçoise*

Smoked mackerel is a regular visitor to both of our fridges. Full of good fats and omega 3s to make us brainier and our eyes brighter (if you believe all that stuff), it's wonderful whipped up into a quick paté with some cream cheese, paprika, lemon juice and black pepper. It responds well to a light grilling too and gives a smoky and rich warmth to this remake of the classic tuna niçoise.

```
Serves 4

6 small waxy potatoes
1 medium beetroot
2 handfuls of green beans
4 slices sourdough bread
Olive oil, to drizzle
4 smoked mackerel fillets
4 medium free range eggs
2 spring onions, chopped
Handful of parsley, finely chopped

Dressing
3 teaspoons creamed horseradish
Juice of 1 lemon
1 tablespoon olive oil
Salt and pepper
```

Cook the potatoes in a pan of boiling water for 15 minutes. Peel and grate the beetroot into a large bowl and mix all the dressing ingredients together separately.

Add the green beans to the potatoes for the last 5 minutes of their cooking time. Drizzle the sourdough with olive oil and place under a hot grill with the mackerel fillets for 5 minutes, turning the bread once browned on one side.

Crack an egg into a cup and drop into a shallow frying pan of boiling water. Repeat quickly with each egg then turn the heat off and leave for 5 minutes.

Layer all the ingredients in the bowl with the dressing, being careful not to over toss the salad and stain it too pink with the beetroot. Top with the poached egg, break the grilled bread into croutons over the top and serve.

A fragrant winters lunch for the first blue sky
— *Allspice Buttered Chicken*
— *Pistachio, Sultana and Rose Pilaf with Nigella Lebneh*

Allspice Buttered Chicken

Serves 6

1 large free range chicken, about 1.5kg
100g unsalted butter, softened
1 tablespoon ground allspice
1 lemon

Preheat the oven to 200ºC/gas mark 6 and sit the chicken in a roasting tin. In a small bowl, combine ¾ of the butter with the allspice and rub into the chicken, including the pockets under the breast skin and in and around the cavity.

Zest the lemon over the chicken, then halve it and squeeze one half's juices over the bird. Tuck the used half inside the cavity and roast in the oven for 1 hour 20 minutes, until the skin is brown and crispy and the bird's juices run clear. Make sure to baste it frequently.

Pistachio, Sultana and Rose Pilaf with Nigella Lebneh
The rose petals in this dish come from our local wholefood shop where herbs and spices are sold from help-yourself plastic jars on tall shelves. Buying by weight makes them incredibly cheap – the quantity used here cost a few pennies and are by no means extravagant. There are tons of online retailers selling spices if you can't find them in a local specialist shop, or you could grow your own, free of pesticides, but if you can't find them at all simply leave them out; though they impart a gentle scent to the rice, they are more decorative than flavoursome.

Serves 6

For the pilaf
25g unsalted butter, softened
3 star anise
4 cloves
10 coriander seeds
½ cinnamon stick
350g basmati rice
½ litre chicken stock
2 large handfuls of sultanas
Handful of pistachios, shelled and halved
Handful of rose petals
Handful of fresh coriander, roughly chopped
Salt

For the Nigella lebneh
500ml lebneh (strained Middle Eastern yogurt)
  or thick Greek yogurt
A large pinch of nigella or black onion seeds

Heat the butter in a large pan and add the star anise, cloves, coriander seeds and cinnamon stick. Fry on low for a few minutes, stirring all the time to prevent catching and to release their flavours. Add the rice, stir to coat for a couple of minutes until a little translucent then follow with the stock – this should be enough to cover the rice plus half a centimetre (add more water as you go if necessary). Add a couple of generous pinches of salt, stir the rice once and then leave well alone. Cover with a tight lid, turn the heat to low and allow to steam until the water has been absorbed – around 20 minutes. At this point, scatter the sultanas, pistachios and half the rose petals on top of the rice, turn the heat off and place a clean tea towel under the lid. Keep the rice here until you need it.

When the bird's ready, remove from the oven, cover in foil and rest for 10 minutes. Spoon the lebneh or yogurt into a bowl and scatter with nigella seeds. Stir the rice once with a fork and serve onto a large platter. Sit the chicken on top so that its juices are soaked up by the rice and pour over the gravy from the roasting tin. Squeeze over the remaining lemon half, finish with coriander and the last of the rose petals, then carve and serve with the lebneh and beer (Lebanese Almaza is good, if you can find it!).

Alternative birds
— *Chicken with Lemon and Fennel Seeds*
— *Chicken with Harissa and Coriander*
— *Poussin with Sage and Garlic*
— *Sticky Ginger Quail*

Chicken with Lemon and Fennel Seeds

Fill the cavity with 2 unpeeled onion halves, 4 unpeeled garlic cloves and 2 lemon halves that have been squeezed over the bird. Melt a knob of butter in a pan with a splash of olive oil, throw in 2 handfuls of fennel seeds and fry until lightly browned. Tip over the chicken (getting some under the skin at the neck if you can) and roast as on page 146.

Set the chicken aside to rest and make the gravy. Remove the onion and garlic from the cavity and put them in the tin with the reserved meat juices on the hob. Discard the lemons. Squash the garlic and onions into the juice with the back of a wooden spoon, add one tablespoon of sifted plain flour, stir and turn on the heat. Add a splash of balsamic vinegar and some water. Stir until slightly thickened and put in a jug on the table.

Chicken with Harissa and Coriander

Fill the cavity with a handful of dried chillies and 4 unpeeled garlic cloves. Spread harissa paste over and under the skin and drizzle with olive oil. Cook the chicken as on page 146 and finish with fresh coriander and a dollop of cool yogurt.

See Ellie's quick harissa recipe below or feel free to use a shop bought version.

Ellie's Hot Hot Harissa

Makes 1 regular jam jar, which will keep for a few weeks in your fridge. Cover the top with olive oil to prevent mould.

Plunge 5 or 6 dried whole red chillies in a small bowl of hot water for up to an hour. While they're soaking, add 1½ teaspoon dried cumin, 1½ teaspoon dried coriander seeds and 1 teaspoon dried aniseed to a dry skillet or frying pan on a low hob. Toast for a few of minutes, shaking every now and then, until they turn a couple of shades darker and have released their heady scent.

Cut 2 handfuls of fresh red chillies lengthways (a mix of long and thin, or short and fat is fine, but use whatever's available – markets are especially cheap for making these kinds of easy recipes), and cut away and set aside the majority of the seeds. (To prevent the inevitable pain of rubbing your eyes after handling chillies, work a dash of olive oil into your hands.) Chop the chillies roughly, add to the hand blender bowl or food processor and pour in a long glug of your best olive oil. Add 6 peeled garlic cloves, the toasted seeds, the soaked dried chillies and a pinch of salt. Blend to a coarse paste. Add more oil to loosen if necessary, and any of the discarded seeds if you want to turn the heat up. Transfer to a sterilised jam jar and refrigerate.

Poussin with Sage and Garlic

Put a 25g slab of butter on a chopping board, top with 6 sage leaves and 2 garlic cloves and, using a big knife, roughly chop everything into the butter until it's all mixed together on the board. Rub the butter over and under the skin of the poussin, brown on all sides in a hot frying pan and roast at 180ºC/gas mark 4 for 30–35 minutes, basting once halfway. Rest for a few minutes and then serve.

Sticky Ginger Quail

Quails are tiny little things so we like to allow 2 per person. For the marinade, blend 2 tablespoons of pomegranate molasses, the juice of an orange, a 3cm piece of fresh root ginger, grated, and a tablespoon of ground ginger. Spread over the quail and roast for 25–30 minutes, basting once, until golden brown and cooked through.

Weeknight comfort
— *Sweet Potato, Fennel and Smoked Bacon Gratin*

This is one of those lucky recipes that accidentally came to be when using up the only food in the house after a weekend of entertaining and fried breakfasts, and it has since become a comfort food fail-safe in both our households. Serve with a simple green salad and some crisp white wine.

Serves 6

Glug of olive oil
200g smoked bacon, cut into small strips
2 medium fennel bulbs, finely sliced
2 sprigs of thyme, leaves only
1 bay leaf
3 large sweet potatoes
500ml double cream
100g Parmesan, grated
Pepper

Preheat the oven to 170ºC/gas mark 4. Heat the olive oil in a wide frying pan over a medium heat and fry the bacon, fennel, thyme leaves and bay leaf for about 15 minutes, until the fennel is soft and taking on some colour. Slice the sweet potatoes into thin rounds.

In a rectangular gratin dish or high-sided baking tin, make one layer of sweet potato slices – it's fine for them to overlap. Spoon some of the fennel and bacon mixture over the top, add another layer of sweet potato and repeat until everything is used up.

Pour over the cream, and scatter the Parmesan on top with a few grinds of pepper. Bake in the oven for 35–40 minutes until the sweet potato is soft and the top is golden brown and crunchy. Put the dish on the table and plate-up.

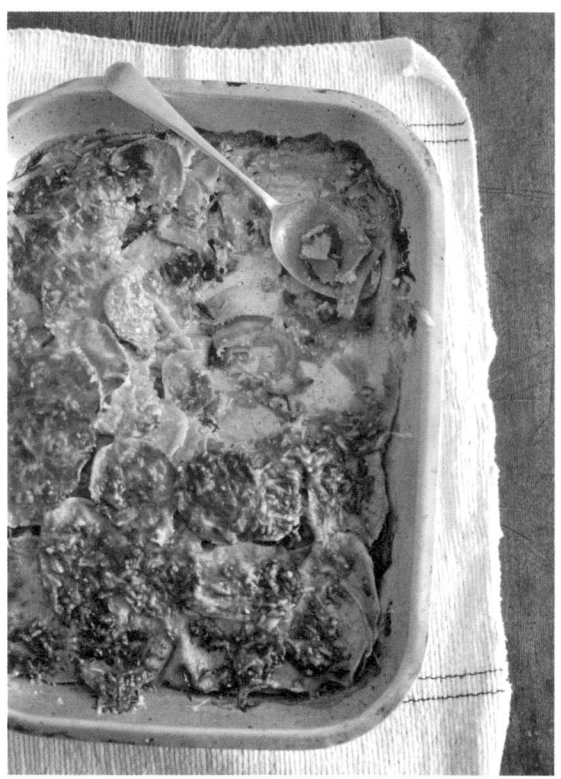

Food for the one you love
— *Melanzane*

Melanzane Parmigiana is a labour- and love-intensive dish. It is best made when you have half a day ahead of you to enjoy cooking and someone (or a group of people) to love and impress. This recipe was given to us by a friend who slaved over a hot stove in her underwear in the heat of a Tuscan July! It was by far the best we've ever eaten.

Serves 4

2 large aubergines
Few pinches of salt
4 garlic cloves, peeled
½ cup olive oil
2 x 400g tins plum tomatoes
1 teaspoon sugar
½ cup sunflower oil
2 balls buffalo mozzarella
Block of Parmesan, for shaving
Handful of fresh basil leaves, for scattering
Green salad and olive bread, to serve

Slice the aubergine into rounds about the thickness of a pound coin. Put them in a colander over the sink, cover liberally with salt and allow to drain for up to an hour, turning occasionally.

Crush the garlic into a heavy-bottomed pan and add the olive oil. Fry over a low heat for a few minutes until the scent intensifies, then add the tomatoes. To get the best flavour out of them, crush them through your hands as they go in. Fill both cans with water and add to the pan along with the sugar. Turn the heat to low and allow the sauce to simmer until reduced by as much as three quarters. It should take about an hour until thick and spoonable. If you have time, allow the sauce to cool and rest for an hour or two as well.

Preheat the oven to 180°C/gas mark 4. Carefully rinse the aubergine slices and squeeze dry between flat palms. Heat a third of the sunflower oil in a large, non-stick frying pan until fizzing. Flash-fry the aubergine in batches until lightly browned, then add a layer to the base of a small but deep ovenproof dish. Spoon over a little of the tomato sauce evenly and follow with torn mozzarella. Keep layering the dish in the same way as a lasagne. Finish with grated Parmesan and bake for 25 minutes. Remove from the oven, let it rest for a few minutes and scatter with torn basil. Serve with a fresh green salad and olive bread.

A rich, meaty meal for a bitterly cold night
— *Salted Pork Belly Stew with Black Pudding, Chorizo and Butter Beans*

This is an exceptionally rich dish that provides belly warmth to the highest degree and is inspired by the Spanish dish *Fabada*. Smoky and intense, it's perfect for ladling into big bowls, for big groups, with big hunks of sourdough and big glasses of red wine. Adding kale, spinach or cabbage in the last 5 minutes might just bring the richness down a notch or two.

Quality meat makes all the difference and the salt and spices blended in the chorizo and *morcelo* (paprika and cumin, respectively), will bring the stew alive. There's no need for salt and pepper or any extra oil – it all comes from the pork. If the quantity of fat worries you, make the stew a day in advance, refrigerate overnight and skim it from the surface before reheating. Definitely not something to be eaten every day – once a year, when the tips of your fingers can bear the cold no more, should be about right.

Serves 4–6

200g salted pork belly
Splash extra virgin olive oil
2 small white onions, finely sliced
2 fresh bay leaves
4 fresh sage leaves, roughly chopped
220g chorizo picante, sliced into 1cm
  diagonals
100g morcelo black pudding, skinned and
  cut into rounds
2 garlic cloves, finely cut
400g tin plum tomatoes
750ml boiling water
2 x 400g tins butter beans, drained
Handful of fresh parsley

Preheat the oven to 180ºC/gas mark 4. Rinse and skin the pork belly, remove the top layer of fat and cut into rough dice. Add to a casserole with a small splash of olive oil and set over a medium-low heat. Add the onions, bay and sage leaves and let everything sweat for about 10 minutes until soft and starting to colour.

In a smaller saucepan, heat the chorizo on low until it releases its oils. When it is rust coloured, remove with a slotted spoon and add to the pork belly, onions and herbs. Keep everything moving for a few minutes.

Crumble the morcelo rounds into a smaller saucepan and add the garlic. After 5 minutes, pour the plum tomatoes through your hands and into the saucepan, breaking them up as you go. Add the boiling water and one tin of butter beans. Bring up to the boil then remove from the heat.

Wipe the chorizo saucepan clean and add 1 tablespoon of liquid from the stew pot, along with 1 tablespoon of water. Set aside. Cover the stew with a tight lid and place in the oven for 2 hours, or until the pork belly is soft and rendered.

Ten minutes before the end of cooking time, add the second tin of butter beans to the reserved liquid in the small pan. Heat through on low with a small splash of olive oil. Crush the beans to a coarse paste with a fork, spoon straight into bowls and top with ladles of stew and chopped fresh parsley.

Tender beef curry for a crowded table
— Beef, Ginger and Coconut Curry with Coriander Rice

Our curry is similar to Thai massaman curry, a rich dish made traditionally with beef, potatoes and peanuts. The massaman paste gives great depth here but we've left out the calorific peanuts and added some tamarind for a wonderful citrus kick. Everything cooks for a long time so the beef falls apart when teased with a fork and the punchy flavours have time to mingle. We like to be generous with the ginger and use sweet potatoes rather than white potatoes, which thicken the curry and add a lip-smacking sweetness.

This is a great dish to cook for a big weekend lunch or supper when you have the time to relax and enjoy the process. As with all curries, it's even better if left overnight in the fridge.

Delicious served with plain steamed rice or with the vibrant and refreshing coriander rice below.

Serves 8

For the curry
1.5kg braising steak, trimmed of fat
  and cubed
2 star anise
8 cardamom pods, lightly crushed
3cm piece fresh root ginger, peeled and sliced
2 x 400ml tins coconut milk
2 tablespoons tamarind paste (optional)
6 shallots, peeled and halved lengthways
2 tablespoons massaman curry paste
1 red chilli, chopped with seeds
2 sweet potatoes
2 tablespoons fish sauce
Soy sauce, for serving (optional)

For the coriander rice
20g of butter
1 large white onion, finely sliced
400g basmati rice (allow 50g per person)
2 handfuls of fresh coriander, leaves and
  stalks separated and finely chopped
1 tablespoon coriander seeds
800ml water*
Juice of 1 lime
Salt
*We measure the rice in a tea cup and then use the cup to measure out double the quantity of water. It always works for us!

Place the beef in a large flameproof casserole with the star anise, cardamom and ginger. Pour in 1 tin of coconut milk and top up with water until the beef is just covered. Cover and slowly bring to the boil. Turn the heat to low and leave to simmer, partially covered, for 2 hours.

Add the tamarind paste, the other tin of coconut milk, the shallots, curry paste and red chilli and simmer, uncovered, for an hour or until the beef is tender. Peel and chop the sweet potatoes into chunks and add to the pan with the fish sauce. Simmer for a further 20 minutes until the potatoes are cooked and the curry has thickened.

For the Coriander Rice
Melt the butter in a saucepan over a medium heat and add the onion. Fry for about 10 minutes until soft and translucent then add the rice, coriander stalks and seeds and stir gently for a couple of minutes. Pour in the water, add a pinch of salt and bring to the boil, then turn to the lowest heat, cover and leave to cook for 8 minutes.

Turn the heat off, separate the grains with a fork and cover with a tea towel while you lay the table and serve up the curry. At the table, squeeze over the lime juice, and top with the coriander leaves.

This is great served with Thai or Indian beer (which is less gassy and a great foil for spicy food) and with soy sauce on the table for seasoning.

A crowd pleasing pot
— *Ultimate Veggie Chilli*

When you have a mix of vegetarians and carnivores coming over, the last thing you want to do is faff around making two different things. This chilli ticks all the boxes–it's economical, comforting, filling and greedily devoured whenever it's on the menu. A mixture of lentils, pearl barley and kidney beans gives it a really satisfying, meaty texture to fool even the staunchest of carnivores. We tend to have most of these ingredients lurking in our cupboards already so it's great for using things up. Feel free to use any mixture of pulses you like according to what's in your kitchen.

When you're feeding lots of people, you want to join in the conversation rather than be locked to the hob, so try to make this the night before, leave it to intensify and improve for 24 hours, then bring it back to life with a few fresh ingredients.

Serves 6

200g pearl barley
200g brown, green or puy lentils (or
  a mixture)
200ml fresh filtered coffee
3 large dried chillies
Glug of olive oil
2 medium white onions, sliced
1 tablespoon smoked paprika
1 tablespoon cumin
1 tablespoon cayenne pepper
1 tablespoon ground cinnamon
4 cloves garlic, sliced
2 fresh red chillies, sliced and deseeded
2 x 400g tins of chopped (or plum) tomatoes
400g tin of kidney beans
4 peppers (mix of red, orange and yellow —
  optional) Vegetable stock

To serve
Flour tortillas (allow at least 2 per person)
400g grated Cheddar cheese
300ml sour cream
300ml guacamole*
2 gem lettuces, thinly sliced
1 bunch coriander, chopped
Fresh lime halves to squeeze

Preheat the oven to 160ºC/gas mark 3. Soak the pearl barley and lentils in a big bowl of cold water and set aside. Pour the coffee into a bowl with the dried chillies and leave them to soak.

Put your biggest flameproof casserole over a low heat and pour in a glug of olive oil. Add the onions and all the spices, then stir and cook gently for about 15 minutes until the onions are soft and the spices have released their goodness. Add the garlic and fresh red chillies.

Remove the rehydrated chillies from the coffee, slice them and throw them in (seeds and all), along with the coffee. Add the tinned tomatoes, drained barley and lentils and the kidney beans. (At this stage you can also add the peppers, blackened under a hot grill, peeled and sliced. This adds a delicious sweet smokiness but is by no means essential.) Top the pan up with stock until all the pulses are submerged and put the pot in the oven, covered, for an hour to thicken. The chilli's ready when the lentils and barley are soft but still maintaining their structure and bite. Don't let it turn to mush. Season well to taste and serve immediately or leave overnight.

You can serve the chilli with rice if you prefer but we love it wrapped up in tortillas with all the trimmings, or scooped over crispy-skinned baked potatoes.

*To make a quick, fresh guacamole, mash 2–3 avocados together with the juice of a lime, 1 chopped green chilli, chopped spring onions, a pinch of sea salt and a little pepper.

When only batter and gravy will do
— Toad in the Hole with Pancetta and Red Onion Gravy

Most of us hanker after a toad in the hole at some point, and though it's not the most sophisticated of school food hangovers, it's generally remembered with fondness for the comforting batter hugging the cheap bangers encased within. Feel free to use low-grade sausages (they are a peculiarly guilty pleasure, so no judgements cast) otherwise go for quality butchers' sausages with woody herbs.

Serves 4

For the toad
1 red onion, finely sliced
Few sprigs of thyme
125g pancetta, trimmed of fat and diced
400g sausages
250ml red wine
Salt and pepper

For the hole
8 heaped tablespoons plain flour
3 medium free range eggs
½ pint whole milk
100ml groundnut or sunflower oil

Preheat the oven to 220ºC/gas mark 7. Scatter the onion, thyme and pancetta into a large roasting tin and lay the sausages on top. Pour over the wine and a little seasoning. Roast, turning occasionally, for about 30 minutes, until the sausages are browned and the gravy has reduced.

To make the batter, sift the flour into a mixing bowl, make a well in the centre, crack in the eggs and add a dash of the milk. Stir firmly with a wooden spoon, gradually pulling in more flour from the sides of the bowl, until you have a smooth thick batter. Gradually add the rest of the milk, stirring as you go, until your batter is the consistency of double cream.

Remove the sausages from the tin onto a plate and set aside. Pour the onion and pancetta gravy into a saucepan. Don't worry if some of the bits stay in the tin –they'll just become part of the batter. Add the oil to the tin and return to the oven until spitting hot. Return the sausages to the tin, evenly spread out, quickly pour in the batter and return to the oven for 15–20 minutes or until the batter is browned and puffed up.

Heat the pancetta and onion gravy in its pan. Pour over the toad in the hole and serve.

An easy and rewarding belly-warming bowl
— Italian Peasants' Soup or Ribollita

This hearty soup is a tarted-up version of the well-known *Ribollita* of the Tuscan countryside. It's a staple belly warmer when all that you might have in the cupboards and among jars of preserved legumes is beans, cabbage and tinned tomatoes. The soup makes good use of the half-bottle of red we all have hanging around by the hob that's no longer drinkable, but perfectly good for adding to the pot. The inclusion of stale bread, an egg and some pancetta raises the bar of luxury while remaining inexpensive.

Serves 4

2 tablespoons good-quality olive oil,
  plus extra for drizzling
1 medium onion, finely sliced
100g diced pancetta, lardons, or diced
  smoked bacon
1 medium carrot, finely diced
½ leek, cut into fine rings
2 garlic cloves
175ml red wine
400g tin chopped tomatoes
400g tin cannellini beans, drained
¾ litre vegetable stock
½ a medium Savoy cabbage or 200g kale
4 slices slightly stale white bread,
  such as ciabatta or sourdough
2 free range eggs, beaten
Salt and pepper

Warm the olive oil in a flameproof casserole and add the onion to soften. When translucent, add the pancetta and fry until golden, about 5 minutes. Add the carrot and leek and keep stirring. Finely chop one garlic clove and add to the pan, stirring for a minute. Add the wine, simmer for a couple of minutes and follow with the tomatoes, beans and stock. Season and simmer for about 45 minutes, partially covered.

Towards the end of the cooking time, add the cabbage to soften. Rub each slice of bread with the remaining garlic clove, drizzle with a little oil and toast lightly under the grill. Put a slice in the bottom of each deep bowl and spoon over the beaten egg equally. Turn the bread in the egg so that it's absorbed, then ladle the soup straight into the bowls (the piping hot soup will cook the egg), and finish with a little more olive oil.

We also like to add Parmesan shavings, fresh parsley and dried chilli flakes if they're knocking around the kitchen.

An old-fashioned Sunday lunch
— *Gin and Juniper Pork with Leek and Parmesan Stuffed Squash* — *Aromatic Mulled Cider*

Gin and Juniper Pork with Leek and Parmesan Stuffed Squash

We're partial to the odd glass of 'Mother's Ruin' so it follows that our gin habit has found its way into our cooking. Juniper and pork is an age-old combo and the shot of gin in this marinade helps to tenderise the meat and deepen the flavours. It should be cooked long and slow with plenty of olive oil, just as they would in Italy.

Serves 4

For the pork
2 tablespoons juniper berries
1 large sprig rosemary, leaves only
6 sage leaves, finely chopped
60ml gin
4 tablespoons olive oil
2.5kg boned and rolled pork shoulder,
    fat scored
Salt and pepper

For the squash
2 small butternut squash, halved and
    deseeded
Handful of thyme
Olive oil
25g butter
2 leeks, thinly sliced into rounds
4 handfuls of grated Parmesan
Salt and pepper
English mustard and watercress, to serve

Grind the juniper berries, rosemary and sage with a generous handful of sea salt and black pepper in a pestle and mortar. Add the gin and olive oil to loosen.

Rub the marinade over the pork joint with your hands. Wrap in clingfilm and leave in the fridge for as long as you can. Overnight is ideal but an hour or two will do.

Preheat the oven to 220°C/gas mark 7. Unwrap the pork and place on a rimmed baking tin with any marinade that's escaped. Slide the pork onto the highest shelf, fat-side up, and roast for 20–25 minutes until the fat is brown and bubbling. Turn the oven down to 160°C/gas mark 3, cover the joint with two layers of foil and roast for 3–4 hours until the meat falls away when prodded with a fork. If you want guaranteed crispy crackling, remove the foil and turn the

grill on for 5–10 minutes at the end.

For the squash, score the flesh of the squash halves about 1cm deep using a small sharp knife. Fill the empty seed cavities with thyme sprigs and drizzle all over with olive oil and a large pinch of salt. Place on a baking tray and bake in the oven with the pork for the last hour.

Melt the butter in a saucepan, add the leeks and cook for about 8 minutes until tender but retaining some bite.

Take the squash from the oven, discard the thyme and scoop the flesh out of the skin with a spoon, leaving the skins intact on the tray. Stir the squash into the leeks, add some pepper, then tip the mixture back into the squash skins. Top with Parmesan and grill for 5 minutes until browned.

Serve with some fiery English mustard and a handful of watercress.

Aromatic Mulled Cider

These last two winters, having invited a few groups to join us for a run of secret suppers, we wanted to welcome people in from the cold with a steaming, scented cup of something they could carry to the table and continue drinking with their food. The quantities are easy to scale up for big groups and make a welcome change from a heavier mulled wine when you're eating.

Serves 4

1 litre cider
1 apple, halved
8 cloves
2 star anise
1 medium cinnamon stick
10 coriander seeds
½ litre apple juice
Peel of 1 clementine or orange
2–3 tablespoons sugar (or to taste)
2 capfuls of dark rum

Pour the cider into a pan and stud the apple halves with cloves. Add the apple halves to the cider along with the spices and turn the heat to medium. Add the apple juice and cover. Keep the mixture brewing and simmering on a low heat for up to an hour. Test for spice strength and gradually add the sugar, tasting after each addition. When everything's mulled to your liking and you're ready to serve the cider, slosh in the dark rum to act as a boozy throat-warmer.

Quick pastries
— *Chocolate and Hazelnut Swirls*

These are a really quick way to round off a meal along with a coffee. They even serve as an indulgent breakfast in a hurry.

<u>Makes 6</u>

375g ready-rolled puff pastry sheet
3 tablespoons chocolate and hazelnut spread
50g chopped hazelnuts

Preheat the oven to 180ºC/gas mark 4. Lay the pastry sheet onto a floured work surface and roll out into a slightly larger and thinner rectangle. Cover all over
with chocolate spread and sprinkle with the chopped nuts.

Roll the sheet up into a tube from one long end to the other. Cut the tube into 6 evenly sized sections. Turn each section on its side and squash with the palm of your hand into rounds roughly 2cm thick.

Place on baking tray lined with baking parchment and bake for 20 minutes until golden brown.

Feel free to play around with the fillings. Here are some tasty alternatives:

Melted dark chocolate and chestnut purée
Apricot jam and custard
Raisin and cinnamon
Maple syrup and crushed pecans

Quick pancakes
— *Vanilla Pear Pancakes with Hazelnut Mascarpone*

All too often we buy unripe pears in the hope that they'll yield a soft, juicy flesh at a slow and dignified pace. In reality, they'll stay stubbornly hard for a number of days before sinking, rapidly and despondently, into a bruised misshapenness. The useful thing here is that you can use the pears at either end of their ripeness scale – just reduce the cooking time if yours are already on their way out.

Serves 2

For the pears
2 pears, whichever variety is available
1 tablespoon caster sugar
1 vanilla pod, split lengthways

For the mascarpone
Handful of whole hazelnuts
2 tablespoons mascarpone

For the pancakes
1 medium free range egg
75ml semi-skimmed milk
5 tablespoons flour
2 pinches of cinnamon
2 pinches of caster sugar
Pinch of salt
Knob of butter

Peel and core both pears and cut each into 6. Add to a pan with the sugar and vanilla pod and cover with a circle of parchment paper. Cook until softened. Strain the pears and reserve the liquid in a bowl.

For the mascarpone, toast the hazelnuts in a dry frying pan, turning frequently, until a shade darker and then chop them coarsely. Put the mascarpone into a bowl and fold in the chopped nuts.

To make the pancakes, whisk together the egg, milk, flour, cinnamon, sugar and salt to form a batter the consistency of single cream. Gradually add more milk if needed. Melt the butter in a non-stick frying pan and when it foams, ladle in half the batter, making sure to roll it around the edges. Cook the pancake on both sides until golden and repeat with the remaining batter.

Return the pear syrup to the pan and warm gently. Top the pancakes with the pear slices and serve with hazelnut mascarpone and a drizzle of pear syrup.

Top of the pots
— *Chilli Chocolate Pots*

This is just the kind of pudding you could put together from ingredients bought at the corner shop and can be made in advance and refrigerated until needed. Try replacing the chilli with crushed nuts or chopped prunes.

Serves 2

```
60g unsalted butter, diced, plus extra for
   buttering
1 heaped tablespoon cocoa powder
60g good-quality dark chocolate (minimum
   70% cocoa solids), broken into pieces
Pinch of chilli powder
1 medium free range egg plus 1 yolk
60g caster sugar
Pinch of salt
1 tablespoon plain flour
Crème fraîche or raspberry coulis, to serve
```

Preheat the oven to 200°C/gas mark 6. Butter the insides of two ramekins and dust both with cocoa powder. Melt the butter, chocolate and chilli powder in a heatproof bowl over a saucepan of barely simmering water and stir until melted. Allow to cool while you whisk together the egg, yolk, sugar and salt until pale and airy – this is best done with an electric whisk.

Fold the chocolate carefully into the egg mixture followed by the flour. Spoon into the ramekins and refrigerate until needed.

Bake for 15 minutes until the top is smooth and set. Pierce the top and fill with a sharp crème fraîche or tart raspberry coulis.

A quick pudding to round off any meal
— *Four Affogatos*

This is one of the best ways to finish a meal and it also happens to be one of the quickest and easiest. It kills two birds with one stone by avoiding the need to make a fussy pudding while incorporating that end-of-a-boozy-meal coffee moment.

To assemble, make a pot of strong coffee in a percolator or cafetière, or, if you have a fancy coffee machine, line up four espressos. Fill your smallest tumblers with vanilla ice cream, pour over some coffee until halfway up the glass and top with your favourite melted chocolate, nuts or berries. Feel free to play around and omit the coffee for children and the caffeine intolerant.

Hazelnuts Warmed with Salted Caramel
Shop-bought jars of salted caramel are perfectly acceptable but if you want to make it yourself, bring 150g caster sugar and 1 tablespoon of water to the boil in a saucepan over a high heat, resisting the urge to stir or even get close – it can seriously burn. When caramelised and bubbling, turn the heat off and add 50g salted butter, 75ml double cream and a generous pinch of sea salt. Turn the heat back on to low and stir the caramel until smooth.

Crumbled Halva with Crushed Raspberries
Halva can be bought in tubs from Middle Eastern shops and some larger supermarkets. If you can't find it, toasted sesame seeds and pistachios would be a very easy alternative. Simply crumble a slice of halva over your affogato and pinch a few ripe raspberries over the top.

Melted Dark Chocolate and Orange Zest
Melt 125g good quality dark chocolate (at least 70% cocoa solids) in a heatproof bowl over a pan of simmering water and grate in the zest of half an orange. Stir, remove from the heat and pour on top of the affogato. Finish with a little more zest for colour.

Toasted Almonds and a Drizzle of Honey
Toast a large handful of flaked almonds in a dry frying pan until lightly browned. Scatter on top of the affogato and finish with a drizzle of good-quality clear honey and a dollop of double cream.

A flourless and fruity chocolate cake
— *Chocolate, Apricot and Ginger*

This dense, wonderfully moist chocolate cake was a result of a build-up of dried apricots and a lack of flour in the cupboard. It is inspired by the classic combination of chocolate and apricot jam in the Viennese classic Sachertorte.

Serves 8-10

For the cake
Butter, for greasing
300g dried apricots
225ml ginger beer
1 cinnamon stick
Zest and juice of 1 lemon
6 free range eggs
200g ground almonds
175g golden caster sugar
30g cocoa
1 teaspoon baking powder

For the topping
200g dark chocolate
200ml sour cream or crème fraîche
Zest and juice of 1 clementine
Handful of crystallised ginger, roughly
  chopped

Preheat the oven to 180ºC/gas mark 4 and butter a 20cm cake tin. Roughly chop the apricots and put in a pan with the ginger beer, cinnamon stick, lemon zest and juice. Bring to the boil and simmer for 15 minutes until the apricots have softened and most of the liquid has been absorbed. Remove the cinnamon stick, purée the mixture and leave to cool.

Whisk the eggs in a large bowl and stir in the ground almonds, sugar, cocoa, baking powder and puréed apricot mixture. Pour into the tin and bake for 45 minutes. Run a knife around the edge, then leave to cool.

To make the topping, melt the chocolate in a heatproof bowl set over a pan of barely simmering water, remove from the heat and stir in the sour cream or crème fraîche and the clementine zest and juice. Spread over the top of the cake using a spatula and top with the chopped crystallised ginger.

We would like to thank: Jenny Wheatley for her superb direction and support;
Laura Edwards for her stunning photography; Bob for his assistance in Italy
and onwards; Tonia George and Ellie Jarvis for their styling and guidance and
Dave Lane for 'seeing' this book before it was even made. Thanks to you all
for being behind us and for making the creative process so easy!

Thank you to Louise Lamont for believing in us – and for eating with us – from
the very beginning. Thank you to Lino Manocci for kindly having us in his
beautiful house in Tuscany in June and for being such a generous host – those
summer shots are our favourites. Thank you to OFM for awarding us with the
title Best Food Blog in 2010, and for shinning a light on our writing.

Last, but not least, a big thank you to Tom, Raph and our loving families
for their vital feedback and for putting up with our antisocial working hours.
This book is dedicated to you.